Y0-BET-148

Getting a Cut

Getting a Cut

A Contextual Understanding of Commission Systems

Richard Seltzer and
Holona LeAnne Ochs

LEXINGTON BOOKS
A division of
ROWMAN & LITTLEFIELD PUBLISHERS, INC.
Lanham • Boulder • New York • Toronto • Plymouth, UK

Published by Lexington Books
A division of Rowman & Littlefield Publishers, Inc.
A wholly owned subsidiary of The Rowman & Littlefield Publishing Group, Inc.
4501 Forbes Boulevard, Suite 200, Lanham, Maryland 20706
www.lexingtonbooks.com

Estover Road, Plymouth PL6 7PY, United Kingdom

Copyright © 2010 by Lexington Books

All rights reserved. No part of this book may be reproduced in any form or by any
electronic or mechanical means, including information storage and retrieval systems,
without written permission from the publisher, except by a reviewer who may quote
passages in a review.

British Library Cataloguing in Publication Information Available

Library of Congress Cataloging-in-Publication Data

Seltzer, Richard, Ph. D.
  Getting a cut : a contextual understanding of commission systems / Richard Seltzer
and Holona LeAnne Ochs.
    p. cm.
  Includes bibliographical references and index.
  ISBN 978-0-7391-4439-8 (cloth : alk. paper) — ISBN 978-0-7391-4441-1 (electronic)
  1. Wage payment systems. 2. Bonus system. 3. Commission merchants. I. Ochs,
Holona LeAnne. II. Title.
  HD4926.S45 2010
  331.2'164—dc22   2010027784

∞ ™ The paper used in this publication meets the minimum requirements of American
National Standard for Information Sciences—Permanence of Paper for Printed Library
Materials, ANSI/NISO Z39.48-1992.

Printed in the United States of America

Library
University of Texas
at San Antonio

Contents

Preface

This book is the companion volume to *Gratuity: A Contextual Understanding of Tipping Norms From the Perspective of Tipped Employees*. The research project from which this series originated began with a simple interest in compensation structures and how people experience the custom of tipping and commission structures. The perspective of those who receive tips and commissions has been largely ignored, and much of the literature on tips, commissions, and bonuses focuses on the concerns of management without regard for the employees or much recognition that understanding the employee perspective contributes significantly to fostering a more productive work environment.

The data utilized in the two companion projects come from over 450 semi-structured interviews. A variety of techniques were employed to ensure that the sample size in this study is large and diverse enough to make useful generalizations. Detailed notes were taken during the interviews, and the respondents' stories are essentially presented in their own voice. This approach is intended to provide authenticity. More importantly, narratives tell an interesting story that reveals insights that no other method adequately conveys. Some of the respondents commented on customer characteristics such as race, gender, age, sexual orientation, and so forth. In those cases, the relevant characteristics of the respondent were included in the narrative as well when the interviewer knew the demographic characteristics of the respondent to provide the greatest degree of clarity of context.

GETTING THE INTERVIEWS

A variety of mechanisms were employed to find the respondents interviewed in this book and the companion volume.[1]

1. The interviewer walked up to people in streets, airports, parking lots, and other public spaces who had relevant jobs: travel agents, sales personnel, and so on. It was very difficult to talk to people while they were working. Most did not have the luxury of taking ten minutes off to be interviewed while at work. In those cases, the interviewer tried to get their phone numbers. This technique was successful in about half of the attempts, and only about ten interviews were conducted as a result of this approach.

2. Students who had relevant employment were given the opportunity to receive extra credit (or cash) if they were interviewed, or if they could refer someone who consented to an interview. Twenty-five interviews resulted from this technique, and another forty people were referred.

3. Whenever the interviewer came into contact with people who provided a service involving a tip, a commission, or a bonus, that person was asked for an interview. Approximately fifty interviews were conducted in this way.

4. Over two hundred personal contacts were solicited for interviews and/ or referrals when appropriate. About twenty personal contacts were interviewed, and around 150 interviews were referred from personal contacts.

5. Almost everyone interviewed was asked if they could refer anyone else. Approximately 150 interviews by this type of "snowball" were conducted. There were several people who were interviewed in the fifth generation of a snowball.

There were several factors that were integral to obtaining the interviews.

1. *Money*: Everyone interviewed (except students enrolled in one of the methodology courses taught by Seltzer who had the option of participating in an interview to receive extra credit) was offered $10 for the interview and $5 if they could successfully refer someone else to interview. Money clearly talks. People were paid on the spot. If the interview was by telephone, the money (in cash) was sent within twenty-four hours. Each person interviewed received a letter with the cash, thanking them and asking for help in finding additional people to interview.

2. *University Affiliation*: A number of people agreed to talk simply because the research was being conducted by university professors.

3. *Personal Referral*: By far the most important factor in obtaining the interview was referral. The person who had been referred was contacted, and the interviewer would state: "Jane Doe said I should call you." In the typical telephone survey conducted by Gallup or Harris, the response rates are about 25 percent. In this study, there were less than five refusals in the 300 or so people referred and interviewed using this introduction. An additional ten people never picked up their telephone or returned the message. This response rate is extraordinarily high.[2]

Even though the response rate was exceptionally high, ironclad conclusions about people who receive tips, commissions, and bonuses cannot be drawn from this sample. The sample in this study is not a random or representative sample. This study is based on a convenience sample combined with a snowball sample.

Although the sample is not random, it is very diverse. Respondents came from thirty-six states and are very heterogeneous by race, class, and gender. The sample represents a broad range of jobs: clothing salespeople, realtors, tire salesmen, telemarketers, travel agents, employment agents, loan officers, membership directors, and others.

Respondents were promised confidentiality, and all names have been changed. In some situations, the name of the business where the respondent worked is referenced. There are also some situations in which the names of some well-known firms are not mentioned at the request of the respondent. In some cases, the location of the respondent (e.g., Northeast instead of Connecticut) is intentionally vague to ensure confidentiality.

Approximately 450 people across 600 different jobs were interviewed. Obviously, we cannot include all 600 narratives in this book or its companion. Readers who wish to read the archived essays can send an e-mail to rseltzer@howard.edu. There are some situations in which we reference an archived narrative, and we note this by stating that the essay is not included.

This book is divided into nine separate categories to reflect differences in the contexts. The narratives are organized and analyzed according to the following contexts: (1) travel; (2) financial services; (3) realty; (4) agents; (5) direct marketing; (6) clothes, jewelry, and cosmetics; (7) electronics; (8) auto parts, sales, and service; and (9) miscellaneous. These conceptual distinctions are relevant because they reflect differences in the products, services, clients or customers, job duties, professional standards, work environment, and the type of employees attracted to that line of work.

We are grateful to many people who helped bring this book to fruition. The 450 people who were interviewed deserve the most thanks. They gave us their time, and they spoke from the heart. Many respondents also helped by referring additional people to be interviewed. Our families and friends gave us a lot of support (as well as names of people to interview). Seltzer's immediate family (Grace, Mike, and Mat) developed tolerance for his conducting interviews at every opportunity. He dedicates this book to the memory of his parents, who both died as the book was being finished.

The patience and understanding of our family and friends has been invaluable. Ochs would not be able to do her work without the support of her family (Kuroki, Rita, Frank, and Mike). Many friends and extended family were also extraordinarily helpful in finding people to be interviewed. Several colleagues read all or part of the manuscript and gave us many thoughtful suggestions. In particular, we thank Dave Heffernan, Yolanda Curtis, Gary Roth, Anne Lopes, and Hillary Watts Bird. In addition, our editors at Lexington Books, Joseph Parry and Victoria Koulakjian, were very helpful throughout this process.

NOTES

1. For a comprehensive explanation of the methodological strategy employed in this study, refer to the companion volume entitled *Gratuity: A Contextual Understanding of Tipping Norms From the Perspective of Tipped Employees.*

2. See Seltzer (2005) for an analysis of response rates and minimizing non-response bias.

Introduction

A remuneration commission denotes a payment for services rendered or products sold and is a common type of incentive to promote sales and reward salespeople. Markets are driven by motivating sales and increasing exchange, and nonstandard compensation in the form of commissions and bonuses attempt to increase productivity and facilitate exchange. However, understanding how these incentives are perceived and when they actually translate into positive, sustainable production value for the company is critical to calculating cost-to-benefit ratio.

Payments are usually calculated on the basis of a percentage of the sales. Commission rates are often hinged upon the achievement of specific targets or minimum sales defined in the contract. Often referred to as a quota, these minimum sales targets are often moving targets that change by month, quarter, or year. It is most often the owner/manager who picks the type of commission system employed; although more experienced salespeople have more power to negotiate commissions. The following are a few examples of the types of commission systems:

- *Negotiated Percentage of the Sales Price*: The agent's cut is a percentage of the sales price of a given product. When an employer wants to increase the volume of sales, this type of commission structure is often employed. The percentage that the agent receives is a function of professional norms, regulation, and his or her experience and skill in negotiation.
- *The Draw/Drawing against Commission*: The commission is often calculated based on the gross profit. However, a draw against commission may also be calculated on various other cuts, such as net profits, units sold, sales

price, sliding scale, and so forth. This is not a straight commission because the calculation is a function of the amount of money advanced against amounts you are expected to earn in future commissions. Depending upon the language of the contract, a draw may make an agent responsible for repayment of any excess draw upon termination of the contract.

- *Sliding Scale Commission*: The commission is configured as a percentage of the sales price, and higher percentages are paid for higher percentages of gross profit achieved. This commission structure incorporates merit in the form of work effort and experience.
- *Straight Commission or a Commission Based on the Percentage of Gross Profit*: In this system, salespeople earn commissions based on the hierarchical extent to which his or her sales contributed to the gross profit. In other words, an agent earns a percentage of the gross profit in competition with the other salespeople in the firm.

Sales forces are a significant investment, costing companies up to forty percent of sales (Zoltners, Sinha, and Zoltners, 2001). The potential return on this investment is primarily in sales creation. A large, well-trained, and motivated sales force is likely to increase sales and have a substantial effect on profitability. A considerable portion of the sales and marketing budget is likely to be spent on sales staff salaries and incentives. Because an unmotivated and undisciplined sales staff can have a tremendous negative impact on company performance and a highly motivated and skilled sales staff can enhance performance immensely, a commission structure that is the best fit for the sales force is critical.

How do people experience this discipline? Are the commission systems interpreted as they are intended? Do people find commissions rewarding? What are the perceptual distinctions between incentives and rewards? What types of commission structures enhance competition, constrain, and motivate? What is the relationship between the management tool and the management craft from the perspective of the employee?

People vary considerably in terms of their capabilities, experiences, and financial needs. Moreover, these variations are likely to vary not only across individuals but for individuals over time as well. This creates a level of complexity in understanding how to engage a sales force to maximize performance. Motivating sales staff requires knowledge and action at the individual level, but incentive structures are comprehensive, uniform programs. This begs the question: How can a commission structure be designed to provide something for everyone in a given context?

Management craft is where the quality of management is judged independent of the tool (the commission structure). If the tool is used to the benefit of management at the expense of employees, trust is undermined by bad management craft. Reinforcements such as the incentives and sanctions that make up a commission system must be consistent to be effective. Commissions need to be obtainable but not automatic to be effective. And, commissions must be perceived as fair to promote a stable, productive sales force. However, individual circumstances vary, market conditions vary, sales territories vary, productive capacities vary, and consumption is most often finite. People working part-time have a different experience with the commission system, and their perspective regarding the "fairness" of the system is likely to be different from full-time employees. How can a commission system be perceived as fair and credible over time so that employees remain engaged?

When utilizing incentives and sanctions, managers need to be able to determine the difference between a situation in which an employee is not properly trained and one in which an employee is apathetic or simply incompetent. A salesperson whose performance is lagging may be motivated by the incentives in the commission system and may not require sanction if training is what is necessary. A commission system is likely to be enhanced by continuing education and training and may lower the overall cost of the sales force. In order for a training program to enhance the commission structure, there are at least two questions that must be answered. First, management must be able to distinguish a competency problem from the various other factors that may affect sales numbers. Second, a training program that costs less than a higher investment in commissions or one that produces greater gains than a higher investment in commissions is likely to produce greater gains.

Commission systems have to be structured in a manner simple enough to provide a clear set of incentives, yet complex enough so that employees cannot game the system. In addition, commission structures are not independent monitoring systems. Adequate commission structures reward sales in the most straightforward manner possible, while also ensuring that only actual sales are rewarded. Although the commission structure has the potential to lower monitoring costs, it does not ensure quality control. In fact, commissions and bonuses can be too large (see, e.g., Miller and Whitford, 2002). When commissions and bonuses are too large, the efficacy of the incentive is undermined. For example, a very large commission may encourage employees to make false promises to customers to increase sales, which may ultimately undercut the business reputation. Moreover, trust is undermined in all respects—management, sales team, and consumer.

Another issue is when the product sucks. Commission systems hold workers accountable for sales growth largely irrespective of the product quality. In fact, companies may issue higher commissions and more bonuses for the worst products in order to move them. How is this nexus between product quality and commissions experienced by the sales staff? Moreover, how does this affect the relationship with the client and the value of the company from the perspective of the sales staff?

This book is intended to address these questions by analyzing the experiences of those who receive commissions within and across various contexts. Because incentive plans are crucial to attracting and retaining sales staff and have a major impact on the activities and behavior of salespeople, understanding how people relate to the commission structure is integral to calculating the appropriate investment in the sales force. A great deal can be learned by understanding how employees come to their decisions about work effort and job satisfaction, and the perspective of the employee is very useful in determining when fostering competition or facilitating cooperation among sales staff is likely to produce the greatest gains in performance.

This book provides a people-first perspective on what it is like to work for commission. The insights from this study offer a well-rounded understanding of various incentive schemes that can inform economic theory, management practices, and working professionals who may utilize nonstandard compensation. Commission systems are a common technique for managing the twin problems of moral hazard and adverse selection in professions where direct monitoring is inefficient or impossible. Commission structures tend to vary across sectors, sales forces, product lines, and over time in a manner that orders sales professions and socializes the sales force to the discipline. The structure of commissions for entry-level positions serves to weed out those who are not self-starters, who require too much monitoring, who do not like the risk, or who are simply not rewarded by the competition. Advancement is based on producing results, and with advancement comes greater autonomy. However, we find that these results do not accumulate over a series of transactions; rather, people who successfully maneuver commission systems describe themselves as working within a network, building a reputation, and developing relationships. In other words, the longevity of a career based on commissions is a function of becoming adept at capitalizing on relationships in a manner that fosters trust. When the relationships between management, employee, and client are not mutually beneficial, trust erodes. The incentives pervert, and the system is unsustainable.

The narratives in this volume reveal that the experiences people have in commission systems is conditioned upon their individual risk-reward orientation, the attainability of the commissions, and the credibility of management. People who do not like the risk or who do not thrive in intense competition do not advance within the rigid structure of the entry-level commission system. When commissions are not perceived as attainable, the sales force appears to suffer as the most competitive candidates find more rewarding employment.

These stories also reveal much about the complex nature of credible management. A highly effective sales force can end up (perversely and unexpectedly) costing a company considerably as the cost of commissions to the company can increase exponentially. Managers may ultimately have to restructure the commission system to manage costs, potentially undermining the effectiveness of the sales force and giving the impression that management may not negotiate in good faith. Good faith in management affects whether or not people like their job as well as their work effort.

Theory

The principal-agent problem or agency dilemma refers to the theoretical understanding of the management and execution of employment contracts.[1] Principal-agency theory assumes that rational, self-interested individuals enter into contracts under conditions of incomplete and asymmetric information. When a principal hires an agent, the twin problems of moral hazard and adverse selection must be addressed.

The prospect that a party insulated from risk may behave differently than if that party were fully exposed to the risk is what is known as moral hazard. The concept of moral hazard does not imply immoral behavior or fraud. The term describes inefficiencies that are likely to occur when risk is not adequately dispersed. Moral hazard is related to the information asymmetry in that a party that is insulated from risk generally has more information about its actions and intentions than the party undertaking the risk. When an agent, acting on behalf of a principal, has more information about his or her actions or intentions than the principal, the agent may have an incentive to behave in accordance with his or her own interests rather than the interests of the principal, particularly when those interests diverge. The greater the degree of agency or the more limited the ability of the principal to monitor the agent, the higher the probability of a moral hazard problem. For example, when there is no clear means of determining who is accountable for a given project, individuals are likely to behave in accordance with their own pecuniary interests. A principal may attempt to align the interests of the principal and agent by establishing a commission system, particularly in work environments where the problem of moral hazard is most vexing. The problem of moral hazard is minimized by shifting some of the risk to the agent by making the agent accountable for production on a given project or account. The commission is intended to ensure that an agent acts in good faith.

Adverse selection refers to a situation in which a negative result occurs because of an information asymmetry. In other words, products, customers, or employees that are not effective or profitable are likely to be selected when access to information is restricted. For example, private information known only to the individual looking for a job may result in an employer (principal) selecting an agent whose interests diverge considerably from the interests of the principal. A principal may attempt to use a commission system to address the problem of adverse selection as well. For example, if a principal selects an agent to sell products door-to-door (a job that is difficult to monitor), only those agents that actually do the work efficiently and effectively are likely to be able to make enough to remain in that profession. The interests of the principal and agent are aligned by the commission in that the higher the work effort, the greater the profits for both the principal and the agent.

There are various mechanisms that may be used to align the interests of principals and agents including piece rate pay, commission systems, profit sharing, efficiency wages, performance measurement, requiring the agent to post a bond, and the risk of job loss. Some of these mechanisms may be used in combination; though some may not. Obviously, commissions are only one mechanism, but commission structures vary considerably both within and across contexts. Moreover, coordination problems can compound the difficulties of management where authority is diffuse or delegation is ambiguous. Such circumstances have the potential to generate agency slack in which the agent actually works against the interest of the principal (see Kiewiet and McCubbins, 1991). In other words, the agent may minimize the effort exerted on behalf of the principal or actually shift outcomes toward his or her own preferences rather than act in the interests of the company as defined by the principal. Although common agency—where multiple principals may delegate responsibility to an agent—is conceptually distinct from situations in which there may be a collective principal, it is important to realize that these situations may not be perceptually distinct in the minds of the sales staff. It is not uncommon for people working within commission systems to operate within layers of management that may or may not be congruent, and they may also see the company as a collective principal, issuing policies that may constrain them in contrasting fashion as well. The importance of acknowledging this perspective is that it can illustrate circumstances in which opportunity structures are not perceived in the manner intended.

It is also important to note that autonomy is distinct from the concepts of both shirking and slippage described in the preceding paragraph. Autonomy refers to the independent action available to the agent that may be used to benefit or undermine the principal. Slack is undesired behavior that inhibits agency performance; whereas autonomy provided to competent employees acting in good faith with adequate incentives has the potential to enhance performance. Understanding the subtle differences between slack and autonomy reveals a great deal about the relationship between the structural elements of the commission system and the efficacy of the management within that system. Consequently, an exploration of commission systems reveals much about the economic elements of incentives, but examining commission systems structurally or simply from a top-down perspective reveals little about how effectively the system addresses the twin problems and potentially impacts productivity. The vastly understudied perspective of the sales staff exposes when independent action on the part of the agent may benefit the company and when it has the potential to increase slack by discerning the process by which employees translate incentives into opportunities. Narratives provide insight regarding how employees see incentives, how they believe they might take advantage of opportunities, and how the structure and management impact their autonomous choices.

A substantial body of research has demonstrated convincingly that individuals also have pro-social considerations and that economic incentives alone are insufficient (see Camerer, 2003). In fact, societies whose members have pro-social preferences are better able to solve collective action problems, achieving higher payoffs than those societies in which the members are exclusively concerned with their individual, pecuniary self-interest (see Cook and Hardin, 2001). Evolutionary social psychology has been applied to economics to understand these pro-social preferences, and this theory contends that the evolutionary stable strategy is to utilize norms of conformity that reinforce pro-social behavior and punish selfish behavior.[2] Sociocultural evolutionary preferences help us understand the motivation of employees and can inform the development of incentive structures that promote long-term, stable growth.

There is surprisingly little research on the motivation of employees or how the various mechanisms perform as solutions to the agency dilemma from the employee perspective. The management literature tends to focus almost exclusively on managers. There is a tremendous gap in our knowledge of how people experience being managed by various commission structures. In particular, information regarding how specific commission structures relate to the motivation of sales staff is critical to determining best practices within and across contexts.

Management in the public sector is understood in three dimensions (Hill and Lynn, 2008): (1) structure; (2) culture; and (3) craft. While critical reflection, analysis, and logical argumentation are essential to balancing these dimensions in the public sector, management in the private sector is afforded more straightforward strategies because the missions of private organizations are defined by the market as opposed to democratic processes. The structural dimension refers to the formal, legal, and institutional rules authority that define organizational boundaries and functions. The cultural dimension is made up of the symbolic thought and social learning, as well as the attitudes, values, goals, and practices of an organization.[3] The craft of management is an artful demonstration of credibility through competence, trustworthiness, and goodwill. Balancing the dimensions requires the same skills of managers: consistency, clear communication, and practicality. Yet, these dimensions of management apply differently to the public, private, and nonprofit sectors as the structure, culture, and craft vary considerably across these sectors. However, as the public-private distinction blurs with increasing privatization and contracting out of government services, understanding how even straightforward processes can become perverted is exceedingly important. A comprehensive understanding of how selfish and pro-social preferences may be oriented in the three dimensions of management requires knowledge of the perceptual elements of structure, culture, and craft.

We have a lot to learn when it comes to understanding the extent to which selfish or pro-social preferences affect work effort. Do people work harder to make more money, or do people work for a sense of accomplishment? How much does the feeling that an individual is helping others affect job performance and satisfaction? Do commission systems promote productivity in the same way across employees with different preferences? How does the structure of the commission system affect employee motivation? What is the optimal design of incentives in a given context to optimize performance?

A contextual understanding of the experiences of employees working in commission systems may reveal a great deal about what motivates employees and subsequently how to structure incentives to align the interests and motivations of employees with the interests of the principal—a goal that would have the mutual benefit of generating greater stability. In addition, we can learn a great deal about how noneconomic incentives may complement a given incentive structure. Perhaps most importantly, an experiential exploration of commissions provides a reasonable framework for promoting growth, and the people-first perspective attempts to ensure that this growth would indeed be mutually beneficial.

NOTES

1. For a comprehensive understanding of the literature on agency theory, refer to Avinash Dixit and Susan Skeath (2004), *Games of Strategy*, New York: Norton.

2. See Fehr and Gächter (2000) for experimental evidence and Bowles and Gintis (2004) for a thorough theoretical analysis.

3. For an interesting assessment of the culture of Wall Street, see Karen Ho (2009), *Liquidated: An Ethnography of Wall Street*, Durham, NC: Duke University Press.

1

Travel

"Video killed the radio star," and the Internet killed travel commissions. Airlines stopped giving commissions to travel agents in 2002. They wanted to cut out the middleperson. However, the narratives in this chapter reveal that some are still able to make a living (barely) from commissions in the travel industry.

The relevant U.S. Bureau of the Census occupation categories for this chapter include travel agents and tour and travel guides.[1] There were approximately 61,000 (down from 90,000 ten years earlier) travel agents in the United States in 2008 making an average of $36,000 annually. There are an estimated 14,000 tour and travel guides making an average of $27,000 per year. Travel agents help travelers sort through information to help them make the most informed decisions about safe travel and assist travelers in finding the best possible price on travel. They offer advice on destinations; arrange transportation, overnight accommodations, and car rentals; book tours; offer insurance on travel; book cruises; and promote travel packages. Customers also expect travel agents to advise on weather, local customs, safety, legal standards, as well as attractions and exhibitions. Travel agents also provide passports, visas, and certificates of vaccination, information on customs, travel advisories, and currency exchange rates for international travel. Travel agents may work for travel agencies, tour operators, visitor's bureaus, reservation offices, or be self-employed. Although agents face considerable competition from Internet-based travel booking, some travelers still prefer the expertise and specialized service of an agent. Travel agents who specialize in certain destinations, types of travelers, or modes of transportation are the most likely to remain competitive as new technologies have changed this job market.

Candace has been a travel agent for twenty years. This is her story.

I no longer like being a travel agent. It has become aggravating because of changes in commissions. With the advent of the Internet, the airlines began to wipe out commissions. We used to get 10 percent for all airline booking. They reduced this to 7 percent, then 5 percent, and eventually to 0. When we book airline flights, we have to add a service fee. We almost never write airline tickets anymore. There is some percentage in corporate travel, and we can also mark up international travel.

We get commissions on the following sources. We get 10 percent on tour packages, such as cruises. In some situations, the percentage can be 13, 15, or even 18 percent. We have preferred vendors. If we book over $500,000 per year with a vendor, we will get 18 percent. These commissions are reimbursed by the tour company after the tour is completed.

Travelers do not pay extra for these packages. They pay the same if they go through us or go directly to the cruise company.

We also get commissions on hotels. We generally get 10 percent on domestic hotels and 8 percent on hotels overseas. We prefer that the hotel be prepaid. It is less complicated, and we are more guaranteed to get our commission. If we book the hotel with the client's credit card, it can get complicated.

Car rentals give us a 10 percent commission. Train commissions are usually 5 to 8 percent. The Europass commission is 10 percent but can vary as there are many types of Europasses.

There are two kinds of package traveling. Land packages are pre-packaged and include meals, hotels, travel, et cetera. Independent travel is when we book each item separately. It takes much more time to do the latter, and we don't always get all the commissions. Some agents will charge a service fee for their time for independent travel. They might charge between $100 and $250. I don't do that.

The biggest obstacle for travel agents is that people don't realize that the price is the same regardless of whether they book through us or book directly with the company offering the package or the hotel. We also got killed with the ending of the airline commission.

Candace refused to accept payment for her participation.

Barry has worked for the last two years selling packages at a major cruise line. He insisted that neither his name nor the name of the cruise line be used. The following story is what Barry shared about travel commissions.

I like working for this cruise line. It is a good environment. I like working on commission because I basically write my own check. I get paid when I work hard.

I get a base salary of $20,000.

People use our website and put their names down. They might call us directly, or they fill out a brochure. We do no cold calls. Everyone I call has expressed an interest in our cruises. My commission ranges between $31 and $71 for each cabin depending upon the duration of the cruise and the type of room. People basically pay $100 per night per person for the cruises. Most cruises last between 3 and 7 days.

I close on 2 to 3 reservations and talk to 30 or so people each day. I average 50 to 60 bookings per month. Some of the salespeople get close to 200 bookings per month.

We do not share our commissions. I could talk to someone for several hours, and if they call back and book with someone else, I get nothing.

There are no bonuses. There are some competitions within the sales force for iPods and gift certificates.

Larry has been a travel consultant since he retired from working for the U.S. government in 1999. This is what he had to say about commissions in the travel industry.

I've made a little niche. I help people make private travel plans to Italy. These are people who don't want to do tours. I make the bookings. I love this job. I love Italy, and I get to go twice a year. The job pays for my travel passion.

I charge people $90 an hour, but for a typical two-week tour, I will sell at a flat rate of $500 for my time. At a previous travel firm, they would take one-third or one-half of that. Now that I am self-employed, I keep 100 percent of that.

I also get commissions. I get 8 to 10 percent on hotels. Some will ask me to collect the commission in advance, and others will reimburse me when the client pays the hotel.

Guides will generally charge $400 to $600 for a full day. I will get 10 to 20 percent of that. For car rentals, I get 14 to 16 percent.

I sometimes get commissions on trains, and because I get no fee for booking airlines, I will generally charge $35 to $40 for each booking to compensate myself for my time.

Commissions in the travel business are disappearing. Luckily, they are still prevalent for hotels and cruises. They are gone for airlines.

The narratives in this chapter are as limited as the job growth for travel agents. It is difficult to draw too many conclusions from such a small sample, and some of the themes were probably fairly obvious prior to the interviews. However, there are a few lessons about commissions that can be gleaned from this chapter. Perhaps most importantly, it is apparent that although the commission systems are designed to facilitate growth, this does not guarantee a stable job market. Travel agents did facilitate growth in travel, but that growth did not insulate them from changes in market conditions facilitated by technological advances. Another lesson that these narratives make clear is that commission systems that are highly competitive narrow the playing field, and the best long-term earners learn to specialize. Specifically, when the travel commissions are conceptualized in categories, the advantages are evident in the narratives. We examined commissions for general travel arrangements, cruise packages, and specific destination travel. Travel agents with a diverse range of general accommodations planning have lost revenue to technology that has made it more difficult to demonstrate the value of the service they provide. According to the travel agents interviewed, people may not know that using a travel agent does not cost the traveler extra directly, or they may prefer to make their own arrangements as the time it takes to assess the options is substantially improved through Internet searches and booking. Moreover, industries like the airline industry have cut costs by eliminating commissions all together and increasing incentives for online booking. It also appears that the Internet has served an advertising function for cruise lines but travel agents remain integral to selling and booking cruises. And, travel agents that specialize in an area and guide people through the experience have commissions that are not only unthreatened by new technology, but their jobs have been made more efficient and their autonomy increased as well.

These narratives also highlight the need for future research to explore the impact that new technologies have on the pro-social elements of economic exchange. The social advantages of face-to-face communication in negotiating mutually beneficial contracts (see, e.g., Axelrod, 1984; Valley, Moag, and Bazerman, 1998) and managing conflict (see, e.g., Loomis, 1959; Drolet and Morris, 2000) are well-established. What remains unclear about face-to-face communication versus the computer interface as it relates to commission systems is the extent to which the Internet not only reduces travel commissions but may also decrease the kind of face-to-face interactions that diminish conflict. For example, have the airlines dealt with more conflict that may have previously been inhibited or absorbed by travel agents as more travelers attempt to book online flights?

NOTE

1. As with the companion volume, for most occupational categories we note how many people were employed in that occupation and the corresponding median income. In the companion volume, we used data from the 2000 Census. In this volume, we use data from the 2008 American Community Survey. To improve readability, we round the data to the closest thousand.

2

Financial Services

People with financial jobs have been glamorized in popular books and movies. The Oliver Stone classic, *Wall Street* (1987), epitomizes the popular conception of work in the financial sector. Depictions of big game hunters in an urban jungle wrestling for status among fierce competitors abound. Financial advisors leverage their information advantage to increase their wages, rely on their reputations to sustain their careers, and their ethics are bound by the context they work within. To the extent that the dog-eat-dog portrayal of people working in financial services is accurate, it arises from the commission structure for salespeople in financial services in conjunction with the prevailing culture in those occupations. So, what do these employees get when they've "bagged the elephant"?

There is considerable variation across the financial sector in terms of commission structures, earnings, work environment, and professionalism. Not everyone in the financial sector makes a fortune, and the culture of the occupations is not necessarily consistent with the popular conception captured in the movie *Wall Street*. This chapter attempts to develop an understanding of the experiences of those who receive commissions for their work in the financial sector. The occupational categories relevant to this chapter include:

- securities, commodities, and financial service sales agents;
- loan interviewers;
- loan counselors and officers;
- insurance sales agents; and
- marketing and public relations representatives.

The Census reports that there are approximately 300,000 securities, commodities, and financial service sales agents in the United States making an average of $70,000 annually. There are around 459,000 insurance sales agents with an average annual income of $49,000. The estimated 110,000 loan interviewers in the United States make an average of $36,000 annually, and around 292,000 loan counselors and officers have an average annual income of around $50,000. Marketing consulting services account for approximately 123,000 jobs in the United States, and marketing representatives make an average of about $52,000 annually.

Brokerage commissions for financial services like mutual funds, commodities, loans, securities, and so forth are engendered when the product is bought or sold on the market. Despite estimates that mutual funds, for example, pay over $1 billion dollars in commissions annually, there is surprisingly little research on the commissions paid for mutual fund brokerage.[1] The Securities and Exchange Commission (SEC) requires that individual funds report the actual brokerage commissions, which are included in the statement of additional information for investors; although this report is only sent at the specific request of the investor(s). Moreover, brokerage costs are not often reported in fund guides. This leads to a number of interesting questions about a sector that yields a tremendous amount of money. What is the commission structure? How do commissions relate to performance? How is service evaluated? Do commissions in the financial sector attract and retain the most competent and highly motivated employees to the leading edge of economic growth? Are the notorious words of Gordon Gekko true? Is greed in fact good? Does greed in fact work?

SECURITIES, COMMODITIES, AND
FINANCIAL SERVICES SALES AGENTS

There is a tremendous amount of variation in commission structures for securities, commodities, and financial services sales agents. The commission structures can vary by the type and value of the product, according to the qualifications and expertise of the sales agent, based on the competitiveness of the market, and across agencies. In this sector, the commission structure is intended to incentivize product lines, motivate employees, and manage entry, exit, and advancement in the profession.

Daniel sells loans for E*trade. He has also sold computers for Dell, and his experience receiving commissions from Dell is included in the chapter *on electronics sales and services. The following narrative details Daniel's perspective on commissions in loan brokerage.*

I've been working at E*trade for six months. People call me, call the 800 number for E*trade, fill out an application online, or use Lending Tree. I review the initial application and talk to them. Most applications are "express," where the appraisal is done online. If it is not express, I will do the origination and send it to a processor, underwriter, and title person for review.[2] I generally like my job. I am paid well for my effort. I get $8.66 an hour as a base as well as full medical benefits and a 401K. My commission is based upon a tier system. For each loan I generate per month up to 20, I get $30 each. For 20 to 30 loans, I get $60 each; 30 to 35 loans—$80 each; 35 to 40 loans—$100 each; over 40 loans—$120 each. This is for loans actually borrowed on lines of credit actually established. Last month I sold 38 loans, and the month before I sold 44 loans.

There is also competition within the office which is based upon dollar amounts. There are 25 people in my office. The top seller gets $500. Number two gets $400, and number three gets $300.

We are trying to get more loans out of Lending Tree. Therefore, if 10 percent of the Lending Tree applications get converted to a loan I get 20 percent more in my commission check. So, for 35 loans I would get $100 each (which is $3,500) plus 20 percent of the $3,500 ($700) for a total of $4,200.

The commissions are very obtainable. The loans range in size from $7,500 to a million dollars. They are all home equity or lines of credit based upon home equity. If someone increases their home equity from say $10,000 to $15,000, that counts as a new account.

In an average month, I get 200 applications from Lending Tree and another 200 applications from phone calls and our own Web site. Probably 10 percent come to fruition if I am doing well.

There is no stealing of commissions. Your name is on the file. However, we have a huge turnover. The general atmosphere is a constant push, and it is very stressful. One loan can make or break your ability to pay the rent. People see this job as a stepping-stone. In this department, the person with the most longevity has been here for one year.

There are ways you can take advantage of the rules. You might put an application into process even though you know it won't come through.

*Cheryl has been working at E*trade for four years. This is her story.*

I like working here. The work is challenging, and the people are great. I am a project manager. Our team puts out new products and works with infrastructure. I get paid salary and bonus. My base salary is $109,000.

My bonus is based on three factors: a performance review, the grade level, and my rank against my peers. At my grade level, I am eligible for a bonus equal to 20 percent of my salary. Last year I got 18 percent. At higher grades, the potential percentage is higher—for example, 30 percent.

The actual pool of bonuses is also affected by the company performance.

I have a meeting with my manager at the beginning of the year, and we set my goals for the year. At the end of the year, we discuss my job performance and how I met my goals. I get a lot of feedback. That works OK.

Don't send me the $10.

John is an option trader for currencies in the 4X market. This is his story.

I like it. It is a lot of action and excitement.

The client is charged 10 percent commission on each trade. For a $10,000 trade, $750 goes to a clearinghouse which actually does the trade and $250 goes to my firm. I get 60 percent of the $250 ($150).

The trading can be fairly complicated. The client is betting that the currency is going to go up or down. If it goes in the direction he predicted, he can make a large sum of money. He can also lose quite a bit, and part of what I do is recommend to him how to manage his risk. Sometimes you cut your losses.

You want instability in the market. If the market does not move, the client will lose. The "American option" allows the client to sell at any time and limit your losses. The "London option" does not allow you to trade until the date of expiration. There is no margin allowed in the futures market, so you cannot lose more than you put in.

I get clients because I give full advice. I develop relationships. I am honest. If the person is losing money, I will let them know on a regular basis what is happening. I give a lot of advice and have to be honest. I always take a lot of notes in case of lawsuits. I have never had to go to arbitration or send money back to a client.

The average account starts at $7,500 for the first trade. The person must have $100,000 in our non-interest bearing account, have a net worth of over $2 million and an annual income of over $250,000. My average client had $250,000 to $300,000 active at any one time, and I had twenty-five to thirty clients.

We have junior brokers who make the equivalent of cold calls. Because of the Do Not Call Registry, these cannot be actual cold calls. The client-to-be usually answers an advertisement in the paper or from an e-mail. If the person expresses interest, a more senior trader will go through an extended discussion with the client.

Although you make a commission on each trade, you are not allowed to churn or flip trades. I would not take more than 17 percent in a month of what the guy has invested in the market regardless of his profit. I will charge less, and my clients obviously like that. You can catch more flies with honey than with vinegar.

The most I earned in commissions in one month was $300,000. A lot of it was timing. There were a lot of new currencies being introduced.

When I first broke into the business, I made 500 dials a day. These came from leads that the company purchased. I would talk to someone 10 percent of the time. About 1 percent of the 500 would want a packet sent. I would call a week later and probably open up 10 new accounts a month. As I got bigger, all my new clients came from referrals. I would give a discount on a commission to someone who gave me a referral.

The company has the biggest problem in getting leads. They spend $300,000 a month for leads. They have 70 guys making 500 calls a piece per night. It is hard to develop that many leads. They get leads from Internet ads and e-mail blasts. It is hard to maintain and de-dupe the lists.

The hours and stress on the job are killers. I work eighty to ninety hours a week.

Kramer owns a firm which specialized in pensions, planning, and investments. This is what he had to say about commissions.

I have 11 employees and 1,500 clients. I've been doing this for twenty-five years, and I like it a lot.

My salary is 100 percent commission based. Most of our business is what is called open-architecture. We usually have a 1 percent comprehensive wrapper. If someone invests $100,000, I get 1 percent per year (called 10 points). This covers all transaction costs associated with our firm. The wrapper can vary. If you invest $1 million, the wrapper is usually 4/10 of 1 percent. Most of our income is based upon the wrapper which the SEC calls a commission. I get 80 percent of the fee/commission, and the firm gets 20 percent. At most firms, it is probably closer to fifty-fifty. However, I am senior, and I have very large accounts.

We also sell life insurance and long-term care. For these, we get 50 percent the first year and 10 percent each additional year.

I usually meet with clients once a year and act as their advocate if they have a problem with a claim.

We have our own broker and do not charge beyond the 1 percent wrapper.

We also do estate planning. I usually charge a fee based on $250 an hour or usually around $2,500.

If we invest your money in a mutual fund such as Vanguard or T. Rowe Price, they get their own fee which can vary but is often 4.5 percent. Our company gets 7 to 10 (7/10 of 1 percent to 1 percent) points back from the mutual fund companies. This fee can almost equal the wrapper fee and is a legal referral fee. We tell the client upfront (called unbundling) how this structure works.

The bonus that each associate can make is based exclusively upon retention. A senior manager with ten years of experience will have a base salary of $100,000 to $125,000. They can add 25 percent to that in terms of bonus. One hundred percent get some type of bonus, and the average is 10 to 15 percent. We are looking for 80 percent retention. If you get more than 80 percent retention, you will get your full bonus and some other perks such as a weekend getaway, and so on.

We are all service-oriented. We don't get paid unless the client sticks around. All my clients are by referral. I used to do cold calls, which other associates still do.

Kramer refused the $10 payment for his participation.

Rachael is a relationship manager for hedge funds. She works for a bank in New York City and shared the following story.

I've been doing this for ten years, and I am leaving. I do not like my job. It is difficult working for the bank. They are too disorganized and understaffed. It is hard to do a good job.

Hedge funds are mutual funds that are unregulated, and the returns can be higher and riskier. It is for people who are very rich or for large institutions. The minimum investment is $1 million. Some have $500 million in the hedge funds.

My commission is based upon expected new revenue to the bank. I really don't know what my commission rate is, and it does not affect the decisions that I make. It is like gravy.

It is the hedge fund that pays for services to the bank and not the investor. The bank gets something for each transaction, and I don't know what that amount is. The investors are not paying. It is the hedge fund.

I manage fifteen hedge funds that range from $50,000 to $6 million per year in transaction fees to the bank. We want to weed out the smaller ones.

My commission is based upon new business. My salary is $112,000 per year, my commission last year was $15,000, and my bonus was $30,000. The bonus is totally random. It is a huge mystery. It is based upon the performance of the bank. You really have to screw up not to get your bonus. By Wall Street standards, this is a very small bonus.

Don't send me any money for this. I was glad to help.

Brian became a banker after bussing tables for several years. His experiences receiving tips for his work as a busboy are included in the companion volume on tipping norms. The following narrative details Brian's responses regarding commissions in the financial sector.

I work at an in-store bank. This is a bank inside a grocery store. It is not a traditional bank. All the employees of the bank can open accounts, setup home equity lines, etc. We can do everything from our computer.

For every product we sell, we get points. If we sell over 25,000 points per quarter, we get 4 cents for each additional point.

If we open a checking account, we get 100 points immediately and 300 additional points if it remains open through the quarter. A credit card gives us 50 immediate points and 500 additional points if still open 90 days later.

For home equity lines, we get 2.5 percent of the full loan value. Therefore, a $100,000 loan nets us 2,500 points. Business credit cards are 1,000 points, and certificates of deposit are 50 points and 2.5 percent of the total CD.

I am paid by the hour. I started at $9.00 an hour with no experience. That was great. After 15 months, I make $9.63 an hour. I am moving up to became a "senior banker" at another location and will get $11.85 an hour.

Last quarter I had 40,000 points. My bonus check was $500. I typically get $650 for my hourly wage every two weeks. Depending upon how hard I work, I get $500 to $1,000 per quarter added on.

There are also group bonuses based upon the number of checking accounts that are opened and stay open. In our branch, we are supposed to open and keep open 75 checking accounts per month. If we do that, our bonus is increased 40 percent. Therefore, if my bonus is supposed to be $500—and if our branch opens 75 checking accounts—I get $700. If we open 85 to 90 accounts, we get 50 percent added on. For 90 to 100 accounts, we get 60 percent, and anything over 100, we get 70 percent tacked on. These are called Tiers 1, 2, 3, and 4, respectively. We have been Tier 4 for the last four quarters. A bonus of $500 actually netted me $850 ($500 x 1.70). The manager of the branch makes additional bonuses if we meet these quotas.

I like this system. It is a little unfair that some people who started after I did got a somewhat higher hourly salary, but the system works.

Amos sells annuities in Houston, Texas, and shared the following story.

I sell equity index annuities that are based on the stock market as a whole. People cannot lose money by investing with us. Annuities can be five years or ten years. We are an investment company.

I am paid straight commission. If the person is under 50 years of age, I get 10 percent; and if they are over 65, I get 8 percent. A typical investment would be $100,000 to $500,000. Sometimes it is $1 million. On $100,000, I would get $10,000 as my commission if the person was under 50 years of age.

We have a three-step process. First, we send out packets to people in the area based upon census data. We ask them if they want to save on their social security and save on taxes. Their income is tax deferred. About 10 to 15 percent will call us.

In the second phase, I will meet with people to give an initial presentation. In the third phase, I will sit down and go over investments and give them a proposal. Of those who call us, about 3 to 5 percent will do something. In a typical month, I will make $25,000 to $30,000 in commission; although I aim for $40,000 to $50,000.

Those most likely to do something are paying a lot of taxes on their social security and have lost before in the stock market. There is no useful stereotype based upon age or gender on who will buy.

I do not share my commission, and my only expense is fuel. The company sends out the cards, etc.

It is a good business. I am educating people on wise investments and helping people who are in retirement.

Janet is a financial advisor for a large financial company on the West Coast. She wanted to make sure that her name and the name of the company she worked for would not be used. The following details her responses.

I help manage assets for people with large estates or for retirement purposes. I've been working here for two and a half years, and I like it a lot. I like working with clients. It is fast paced, challenging, and has a mix of work.

I get commissions only. However, I do get health insurance and a 401K. I'm paid a percentage of the assets invested. The typical commission ranges between 3/4 of 1 percent to 2.25 percent. It depends upon the style of investment and the amount of assets. My typical transaction is $50,000 at 1.2 percent. Therefore, the commission would be $600. This would be split with the company. The typical split for new agents is 50 percent. Therefore, I would get $300. I would get this every year for which the account is active.

Agents who have been there longer get a smaller percentage—about 40 percent. This helps out the new agents. Because they have assets that have been there for many years, their total take is far larger. A typical agent in her second year would have $30 to $35 million in assets and get half of the $100,000 to $150,000 commission. A more senior agent will take 40 percent of $600,000 to $700,000 in commissions. Their accounts accumulate year after year. It's exponential.

Most of my business is by referral. I also network at events and seminars. I make a lot of cold calls. I probably get success between 10 percent and 40 percent of the cold calls that I make. Success is measured by having a meeting with the prospective client. Once I meet a prospective client face-to-face, my success rate is probably 60 percent.

It is fairly competitive among younger brokers. It can get nasty, but it is mostly positive. Each office is different. We are fairly supportive of each other in the office. We are hands-off when dealing with each other's clients. Sometimes another agent will give me a lead.

There is a lot of turnover. When someone leaves, his or her accounts are distributed to the other brokers dependent upon a power-ranking system. Those who have more sales get more of the business. It is really an exponential business.

We have partnership levels. There are many different ways that this works. You can buy in or work off your partnership. When you are partner you get a percentage of the business as well as your commissions. At some point, you either become partner or you leave.

You have to be always selling. It is not for everyone. It can really crack you. Sometimes I work sixty hours a week and other times thirty hours.

We like to say that we are fee based and not commission based.

Landon worked for Merrill Lynch for six months. He shared the following story about his experience with commissions.

It was an opportunity to make an awful lot of money and to retire early. However, it would have been at huge personal cost. A lot of people there are in their third or fourth marriage. It is pure capitalism—survival of the fittest. You have no life. The senior manager would come in every morning and tell us that we were losers because we were not bringing in enough money.

My starting salary was $45,000 plus bonuses. My bonuses could have reached $140,000 to $150,000 per year. The bonus, if you get it, could be up to $40,000 a year in cash and the opportunity to buy $100,000 of company stock at 15 percent discount.

The bonus is dependent upon how much liquid capital you acquired. You are expected to get $15 million within 18 months. This needed to be broken down into different categories: mutual funds, fee based, IRAs, stocks, etc. If you reach your target, you get your bonus, and more importantly, you get to keep your job.

You do a lot of cold calls and a lot of cold walking. Cold walking is going to commercial parks and trying to talk to people in stores, and so on. You also occasionally get to be broker for a day. This is when someone calls Merrill Lynch—you talk to them. You also go through phone directories, drive through affluent neighborhoods, look at tax records, etc. Before you call, you need to make sure they are not on the Do Not Call Registry and also check against our own database to make sure they are not someone else's client. You can make up to one hundred calls a day, and from that, you try to get five appointments. Your hope is that one of these will pan out.

I never really made it that far. I called twenty or so a day. Most of these were people I knew. I never got much business. I finally realized that I was unwilling to work one hundred–plus hour weeks. It was not going to make me happy.

There are two basic payment systems. Fee-based is that a person has an account and pays 1.5 percent to 3 percent per year to service it. Commission-based accounts are that someone pays up to 5 percent every time a trade occurs. With commission-based accounts the broker spends more time and gives it more attention. Fee-based accounts have less risk, and money is usually placed in mutual funds. As an investor, you should do fifty-fifty between these two accounts.

The actual percentage that I receive of the fee-based or commission-based account would have been determined by my agreement with my manager. Everyone has a different deal with their manager. It is usually a sliding scale with the broker getting around 20 percent.

The work is like a hustle described in the movie *Boiler Room* or in the book *Liar's Poker* by Michael Lewis (1989). In that movie, a character talks about how black kids sell crack and white kids sell securities. The hustle is the same. You have no friends. You can talk sports, but you don't trust the other brokers.

What you aim for is having a "book." A book is your own group of clients. As your book increases and your bonuses increase, your salary stops. The base salary is only meant to tide you over till you develop your book. If you get recruited by another brokerage firm, you take your book.

I now work where I get paid every two weeks doing financial consulting. I get paid $53,000 per year, only work a forty-hour week, and have much less stress.

Landon refused the $10 payment for participation.

The narratives of the securities, commodities, and financial services agents reveal some patterns that contribute to our understanding of the use of commission systems as a management tool. The structure of the commission system orients competition. The turnover mentioned by several of the interviewees indicates that commissions serve to manage adverse selection. Some jobs are "stepping-stones" where people pay their dues making cold calls, sharing commissions or taking lower percentages compared to senior sales associates, developing their own books to prove that they are self-starters. Those who can't hack it get out or get *pushed* out. In essence, these narratives suggest that commission systems in this context work as they are intended for the most part. However, the process by which they operate is not exactly consistent with theories of economic transactions. People working in this sector describe their economic exchanges in terms of relationships. They develop reputations that they rely on to retain clients in a context where "you want instability in the market" to facilitate exchange, but they have to trust that people will continue to play the game. They attract clients by developing relationships with them. When they are forthright, people trust that it is in their interest to continue playing volatile markets and that information asymmetries are not being used to the exclusive advantage of the agent. They retain clients when the relationship is mutually beneficial rather than simply a transaction that pays off.

It is also interesting to note that commissions are not described as motivating performance. The respondents portray themselves as thriving on the action, excitement, and competition. Entry level commission structures reward people who respond to the challenge and risk, and those who advance in the field depict the commission as though it is "like gravy." Having the most competitive people at the leading edge of market growth in the financial sector facilitates growth, but perhaps the more important factor is that the relationships that they have developed to get to the leading edge foster the trust necessary for sustainability. However, as recent fiascos such as the Bernie Madoff scandal (among numerous other Ponzi schemes that contributed to the collapse of the sector) have shown that greed is not always good, and reputations are best developed from results. Greed only has the potential to be good when it is transparent and produces mutually beneficial gain.

LOAN INTERVIEWERS, COUNSELORS, AND OFFICERS

Most loan officers are employed by banks and typically specialize in commercial, consumer, or mortgage lending. Loan officers are responsible for soliciting loans, represent creditors to borrowers, and vice versa; whereas loan counselors are responsible for guiding potential applicants who tend to have difficulty qualifying for traditional loans through the lending process. Both loan officers and counselors rely on loan interviewers and clerks to elicit information, investigate the backgrounds of applicants, verify references, and prepare loan requests. Although career opportunities as a loan interviewer, counselor, or officer are subject to general economic conditions, economists with the U.S. Bureau of Labor Statistics suggest that through 2018 jobs for loan officers are expected to grow as fast as the average for all careers and that jobs in loan counseling are likely to grow faster than average. Job growth in this sector is expected to stem from increases in the number and complexity of loans.

Recently, lending practices have come into question as perverse incentives to profit from the inability to pay came to dominate the larger lending market. While small banks and cooperatives have maintained stability, large lending institutions have experienced a crisis of credibility. These differences in incentive schemes are also likely to be evident in the commission structures.

Richard has been a loan processor for the past three years. This is what he had to say about commissions in financial services.

I love my job because I get to work with my stepdad, and I like solving puzzles. Each loan is different, and I like helping people.

I have three sources of income:

1. I get paid $15 an hour.
2. For each loan I finish, I get $25 from the loan officer, and the company also gives me $25 as a bonus. However, if the loan officer is my stepdad, he gives me $100 instead of $25 because I am doing some of his duties as a loan officer.
3. When the loan officer is my stepdad, I also get 7.5 percent of his fee.

The loan officer negotiates the terms of the deal and gets all the documents signed. The processor puts the loans into one of three computer systems, verifies income, and makes sure the rates are correct.

As a processor, it takes me approximately 20 hours of my time over 30 to 45 days to do original loans and 10 hours for refinancing.

The loan officer makes his money on the points. Most of our loans are with people with poor credit, and we get two or three points. If the loan is for $100,000, two points is 2 percent, or $2,000. This is the major source of income for the loan officer. If the refinancing is zero points, he will make it up in processing fees and underwriting fees.

I am lucky that I get my 7.5 percent commission. Most processors do not get commission. We had a recent large loan that gave me the following: an hourly wage of $450, a bonus of $125, and a commission of $800. This was unusually high. On most loans, I get $200 to $300.

We work a lot with title people. There is no monetary relationship between us, referral fees, or sharing of revenues. However, we build relations. If we need something really quickly, we know we can rely on the ones we work with again and again.

Sean is a loan officer in the Washington, D.C., area. The following narrative details his experiences with the commission system as a loan officer.

I've been doing this for fourteen years. I like it a lot. I am very richly compensated. It is intellectually challenging, and the work is very fluid.

I am now a part owner, so I also get some of the profit. However, most of my income is from commission. The commission in my industry ranges from 50 to 70 percent. If someone helps you develop the leads, such as using ads or telemarketing, the commission rate is lower. If you are using your own contacts and referrals, the rate is higher. I have a book of business, so my rate is higher. The company is paying less overhead in developing the leads.

I try to find the best price for someone purchasing a mortgage. If it is a high mortgage, that is fairly easy. Let's say $500,000—we would take 1 percent ($5,000). I would get 70 percent of that or $3,500. For mortgages of $100,000 or ones that would take more time, we would take at least 2 percent.

We charge a flat rate of $500 for a line of equity account and do this mostly as a service. I would get $200 for this. Some companies focus on the second mortgage. We don't.

The loan processor (who oversees most of the paperwork) gets a salary ($30,000 to $45,000) as well as a "spiff" of $75 per closing. The spiff is sort of an incentive. The spiff comes from the company side. Some companies have sales managers who would also get a percentage. We don't.

I cultivate people who give me referrals. These could be attorneys, realtors, CPAs, etc. I am not allowed to give them a referral fee. I show them that I can help their clients. Legally, I can take them out to lunch to discuss business or to a ball game for such a discussion. I cannot just give them tickets. The law is being enforced more aggressively now.

Like any kind of sales job it is hard to judge who will be successful. It is a time-sensitive, high-pressure job. If someone comes in asking about draws and minimum salaries, you know they are not cut out for it. You are like a conductor who must keep everything under control.

Sean refused the $10 for his participation.

Mathew is a loan officer in Ohio. He had this to say about commissions.

We make any type of loan that can be tied to a person's house. That includes mortgages, refinancing, home equity loans, and debt-consolidation loans. We own a telemarketing firm which rents lists that are pre-scrubbed. These lists will include people in certain demographic categories of house type and income bracket who are not on the Do Not Call Registry. If someone is interested, I call them back.

I work on straight commission. There are three ways that I make money. The first is based upon the origination fee. We are the middlemen. My fee is based upon a tier system. In a typical $3,000 origination fee, I get a percentage based upon my monthly sales. This schedule is as follows:

0–$10,000: 25 percent
$10,000–$15,000: 42 percent
$15,000–$20,000: 46 percent
$20,000–$25,000: 49 percent
$25,000–$30,000: 50 percent
$30,000+: 60 percent

This percentage amount all goes to me. If I sell $40,000 of origination fees in a month, I get a check for $24,000.

I also get $500 to $700 for each home equity line that I set up.

Third, I also get an "out-the-back" which is also called a yield spread. If the typical percentage point of a loan is 6 percent and I get 6.25 percent, I get 1 percent of the loan amount. So for a $100,000 loan, I would get $1,000 if the bump up is a quarter of a point.

We used to do more refinancing. There is less of that now unless a person has an ARM [Adjustable Rate Mortgage]. I do more debt-consolidation loans.

I do most of my calls between 7:00 and 9:00 pm. I will make 15 to 30 calls a night. Between 1 to 2 percent of the calls yield success.

William is a commercial real estate loan officer for a large bank. He is based in Florida and shared the following story.

I've been doing this work for six years. I am a loan officer for amounts ranging from $5 million to over $50 million. Most of these loans are for construction of income-producing properties and condominium buildings. I like the work that I do. It is challenging. It is not boilerplate. It takes creativity, and you use a variety of methods to make an attractive deal. You see the deal from plans through zoning through construction.

I earn salary plus a type of commission. I am compared among my peers in the East Coast and the Midwest. If our group is profitable, I am ranked among the twenty other people in my group. If I generate over $250,000 in profit, my ranking will be in the top third, and I will get an additional 40 percent of my base salary. If I am in the middle, I will get a 25 percent bonus. Most of the people in my tier have a base salary of $100,000.

Profitability to the bank is based upon three factors. Let's use a $50 million loan as an example. The bank will make about 2 percent on the interest or $100,000. The borrower will also have to pay an origination fee of 1/2 of 1 percent or $25,000. The borrower will also pay for a variety of services such as setting up accounts ($50 a month), changing the loan from floating to fixed rate, et cetera. The latter charges are encouraged as they do not entail any more lending.

Other banks do their commission structures in different ways. Some will have more base salary, and others will have more on commissions. Some allow you to more than double your base salary, but the base will be lower.

Commercial loans are very relationship oriented. You manage the closing of the loan, and you help administer it. Construction loans can be 12, 18, 24, or 36 months. You shepherd it from day one. The borrowers get money on a monthly basis by putting in payment requests where they show how it will be spent each month. You are not just a loan officer, you are a relationship manager.

There is competition on leads and prospects as well as inheriting existing portfolios of loans. There are occasional words where someone will lay claims and say, "I have worked with this person in the past." There is usually more competition with new hires or when banks merge. It usually does not get ugly.

Over the last few years I originated between $35 million and $96 million in loans per year. Last year I put a lot of time into fifteen deals, and about half of these came through.

The narratives in this section reveal a few themes worth further discussion. It is perhaps most noteworthy to point out how these stories highlight those whom loan officers, processors, and counselors consider worth cultivating relationships with versus those whom they describe only as clients that they most often serve. The respondents describe cultivating relationships with people who send business their way or help them develop their books. They also talk about commercial lending as a relationship rather than a transaction. This is important because it illustrates that the relative value of relationships does not appear to be related to the often cited motivation of helping people achieve their dreams. Respondents often say that they like brokering mutually beneficial deals where people get homes, jobs are created, et cetera. However, they actually develop commercial or professional relationships. For example, paying points is an incentive scheme that encourages loan officers to pursue clients who have traditionally been under-served by the market. However, there were several factors that converged in the recent financial crisis that perverted this incentive. First, lending institutions began making substantial profits extending credit beyond an individual's means to repay by getting a quick return on their investment through high interest rates and fees. Second, loan officers, processors, and counselors who often have long-standing relationships developed over repeated transactions were also seeing increasing profits from pursuing clients who would have to pay points, were approved at higher interest rates, and/or were likely to incur exorbitant fees. In much the same way that we can recognize that we do not have time to stop before we rear-end the car in front of us, many of the people involved understood that this was not a sustainable system of rewards. However, financial systems operate on the expectations of others, so for as long as it can generally be expected that the competition will continue to pursue profits in the same manner, the incentive scheme will reward that same behavior. Cooperation to modify the system of rewards that is profitable at the time is unlikely in a highly competitive environment. Innovation is difficult when profitability appears to be stable, and a collapse of the sector is the likely outcome when these factors converge. While many of the respondents described themselves as being rewarded by the opportunity to help people achieve the dream of home ownership, for example, few acknowledged that their pursuit of financial incentives to help people achieve their dream was increasingly more costly for the least well-off.

INSURANCE SALES AGENTS AND BROKERS

These days you can buy insurance for everything from your life to your legs (assuming you have legs worth ensuring). You may purchase insurance from a "captive agent" who works for a single insurance company. You may purchase insurance from someone who brokers insurance for several companies, or you may purchase some insurance online. And much like the impact on travel agents, the Internet has been a double-edged sword for the insurance industry as well. Insurance agents can increase their efficiency and potentially serve more customers as they are able to get information and process applications online. However, customers may also choose to handle some of their own insurance needs; both of which serve to increase competition among insurance agents.

Roy has been a real estate attorney for twenty-five years and has been doing settlements for over fifteen years. He sells title insurance as part of the settlement process. This is what Roy had to say about commissions for selling insurance.

Most days I like my job. It has its moments. It is challenging. A good part of our revenue stream comes from closings. We do many other kinds of real estate law as well.

People who buy homes or refinance have to buy title insurance. Title insurance is in case there is a defect in the ownership of the home. We write this insurance with one company. For a house that sells for $800,000, the premium for the title insurance is about $2,500. We keep 80 percent of this amount. The more insurance you write, the higher the percentage that you keep.

We have a lot of overhead because of the title insurance. We actually do the title work and the investigation. This can take from five minutes to fifty hours. Nevertheless, about half of the income from our commission on the title insurance is profit.

Almost all firms that do real estate closings have this type of relationship with a title company.

No need to send the $10.

Anne has been selling insurance in the District of Columbia area for twenty-one years. The following narrative reflects her responses regarding commissions.

For most term–life insurance policies, I get 30 to 50 percent of the first year premium and 3 percent for each renewal (ongoing residual). Whole life polices rates are a little higher.[3] The average for both is usually 9 to 10 percent over the life of the policy.

Disability insurance has a similar first year rate (30 to 50 percent), but the renewal commission rate is a little higher—about 10 percent.

For people who are buying investment accounts, I get 3 percent of the total investment for the first year and 1/2 of 1 percent for additional years.

Health insurance is 5 to 10 percent of the policy for every year. The first year is not higher. If someone has a serious health issue, their premium is higher, but my commission percentage stays the same.

I deal with ten to fifteen insurance companies. I get a lot of checks each month, and I have to fill out a lot of 1099s at the end of the year. The commission rates vary a lot. I don't pay much attention to the percentages. Some companies will give you a higher commission percentage. However, they usually can't give you much backroom help or service. I would rather get a lower percentage and get more service.

She would not take the $10 for her participation and said to donate it to a charity. As was the case with all other participants in this study who requested that the money be donated, Anne's money was donated to charity.

Norman has been an agent for a large casualty insurance company in Washington, D.C., for thirty years. This is his story.

It has been very good to me. I like it because I am self-employed and have a lot of independence.

The company says that we get a service compensation, which is really a commission. It's the same. There are a variety of policies that I write.

A typical $1 million house has a $1,000-a-year premium. I get 15 percent ($150) every year.

For auto insurance, I get 10 percent for every year. If the policy was initiated by another agent, I get 7 percent for the first nine years, and then I get 10 percent. I would get these policies if the person had a policy that initiated in another state and moved to this area or if the original agent died or retired.

We have different kinds of business insurance—theft, fire, and liability. This brings 20 percent per year.

Workers' comp brings in 10 percent per year.

We also insure jewelry, hearing aids, computers, etc. This pays 15 percent a year in commission.

You are lucky that you called when I had the book near me. I normally never look at these percentages.

For recent agents, it is far more complex. They have quotas for each product type, and their percentages are lower. They then get bonuses at the end of the year. They call this a scorecard. It is very complex, and no one really understands it.

There are also fidelity and probate bonds. I get 15 percent of these. This is required of executors of estates. A mother became the guardian for a disabled child that had a $550,000 fund. She pays $1,600 a year in premiums. Her original policy was via her attorney for about double that.

We also partner with other insurance companies. We don't sell health insurance or life insurance, but I can write a policy with a partner company. I would get 50 percent the first year, 10 percent the second year, and 2 percent after that. For these kinds of policies, there is a lot of work the first year but very little after that.

There is not a lot of competition among agents of this insurance company. We are not allowed to raid or to do rebates.

I get a check every two weeks. I have to pay expenses. I have a staff that is paid a salary. I used to have a bonus plan to drum up new business, but most of my staff wants a regular paycheck they can count on.

I do not own this business. The real value is its renewal business. This is owned by the insurance company. If I retire or get hit by a bus, I get one year's worth of commissions spread over five years. New agents don't have this benefit.

As I said, if someone retires, his or her policies are spread around to existing agents. This goes mostly to new agents as the company can pay them a lower percentage. New agents get 7 percent for most products. This is like GM [General Motors]. They are constantly restructuring and trying to lower costs. Luckily they have stuck by the agreement they made with me. I have an "at-will" contract and could be given thirty days' notice.

We do our own marketing plans. I am limited to marketing within 150 miles of my office. I pay for marketing costs unless they co-op in which we split the cost fifty-fifty.

Norman would not take the $10 for his participation and requested that it be given to a charity.

Robin is an insurance producer in the San Francisco area. This is Robin's story.

I sell property and casualty commercial insurance. I've been in the insurance industry for thirty years. However, I've only been selling insurance for six years. I like what I do because I enjoy meeting people.

My salary is 100 percent commission. I am an independent broker. I work with literally hundreds of different companies. For a typical property insurance policy, the company we write it with (i.e., Fireman's Fund) will pay my company 15 percent of the premium for every year in which the policy exists. I get 40 percent of that for the first year and 20 percent for additional years. This is a fairly typical breakdown.

For worker's comp policies sold, 8 to 10 percent go to my company. I still get 40 percent of that the first year and 20 percent for additional years.

There is also director's liability, where my company will get 10 percent of the premium.

The size of these policies really varies. I have an eight-unit apartment building whose yearly premium is around $10,000. A large manufacturing plant has yearly premiums of $40,000 to $50,000. A very large company like Microsoft will pay millions for its annual premium on just director's liability. I have one company that has a big auto fleet, and their annual premium is $1 million.

There are really two types of insurance—casualty, which is for worker's comp, general liability, and anything for which you might get sued. The second type of insurance is property—this covers the building, furniture, et cetera.

I have nothing to do with claims. I do sales only.

I get renewals. This is called a book. I have a big book. I negotiated a salary for my first two years, so I could get started. I did not have to repay this as often occurs because I brought a lot of experience with me. I had connections.

I split my fees with no one.

I make a lot of cold calls and work with referrals. I do a lot of community work: Rotarians, Chamber of Commerce, and other charities. You have to be well-rounded. By doing community work, it allows you to network. You must do something outside of the industry.

On cold calls, it takes several calls just to find out who the right person is. Sometimes it is the comptroller, other times the CEO, other times the CFO. I probably make five calls before I speak to the right person. I get appointments about one-third of the time after I talk to the right person. This is an extremely high hit ratio. Of those I meet, 25 percent of the time there is no second meeting because of my choice. I walk away because they are looking for cheap insurance, and I have a certain style. About 10 percent of the time they don't like me. Of the 65 percent that I see for a second appointment, I write policies about 80 percent of the time. I am the top salesperson for my company in California.

You have to know when to walk away.

Robin also requested that his money for participation be donated to a charity.

Sam has been an insurance agent for thirty-five years for a company in Denver, Colorado.

I like my job. It is a good way to make a living, and I also help the people I insure. I am an exclusive agent. I work with just one company. Most of my business is home and auto insurance. I get a flat 15 percent for the first year as well as each year of renewal. A typical policy for a $500,000 home would run between $1,000 and $1,500 per year.

I also do commercial-type accounts. For me, this mostly consists of small apartment buildings. I get 15 percent for the first two years and 10 percent in subsequent years.

I do some life insurance. For term insurance, I get 25 percent for the first year, 7 percent for the second year, and 3 percent for other years. Our commission rate for this is pretty pathetic compared to other companies. For whole or universal insurance, I get 55 percent the first year, 7 percent the second, and 3 percent in subsequent years. Our commission rate is one of the lowest in the country, and I don't know why. For many other companies, their rates are 75 percent to agents who bring in over $10,000 a year in premiums, and it goes up after that.

Our commission rate in general is low compared to independent agents. However, we also have lower overhead. I don't have to pay for computers and computer systems. It is just our life insurance that is out of whack.

There is some competition between agents of our company. There are a few who will be unethical when they give information to the underwriters (who assess the risk of the applicant) in order to have a lower rate. However, this is rare. Most of our problems occur when an agent retires or a client decides he does not want to use the agent any more. The account or accounts would get moved to another agent. Our company decides on how the accounts will be divided. When I retire, I cannot sell my accounts to another agent. I can make recommendations. The system does not work because it is based on favoritism. When someone retires, the company will lose about 20 percent of the book.

We have some advantages over independent agents. The companies they work with might set a quota. If they don't make the quota, the agent would be dropped. This compromises their independence.

Ninety percent of my new business is from referral. It is different now because of the Do Not Call Registry. I built this business with a telemarketer. Every morning he would have four or five solid leads from the night before on my desk. I could close about half of them. That gave me sixty new policies a year. He was paid $10 an hour and a dollar or two for every true lead.

The insurance agents interviewed tend to describe their work as it breaks down into percentages. In insurance commissions, the structure attempts to ensure that agents and brokers retain clients to maintain a steady income. But, they must also pursue new clients to maintain current revenue and increase their income.

There is also some indication that respondents who are under pressure to secure new clients see charities, fund-raisers, and community events as business networking opportunities. There are several interesting facets to this insight. It highlights the overlap between the private and nonprofit sectors. It illustrates the relational aspects of business that transcend the transactional aspects of economic exchange. Perhaps even more importantly, it leads us to at least one question for further exploration. How might new technologies impact the presence of business interests in charitable endeavors? Does increasing competition due to new technologies contribute to more participation by business leaders in charitable events, for example? Or, does the increasing ability of individual consumers to purchase their own insurance online contribute to a decline in volunteerism among business professionals? If there is indeed more networking and fund-raising carried out online, how might this impact the relational aspects of both the private and nonprofit sectors? Future research exploring these types of questions may lend insight into the evolving nature of social systems.

MARKETING AND PUBLIC RELATIONS CONSULTANTS

The primary function of marketing and public relations consultants is to enhance the profile of the clients that he or she represents. This means determining how clients want to be perceived by the target audience and designing campaigns, events, and developing tools to implement the strategies to achieve the desired public perception. Building a network of business and community relationships is integral to executing these tasks, and the consultants who make a living in this line of work tend to have strong interpersonal and communication skills. Their commissions reward their ability to affect how people think about the consultant as an individual and their ability to communicate success in shaping public perceptions of the client organization. The following narrative illustrates how people attempt to shape perceptions positively, sometimes in opposition to their own perception or bias.

Daniel works for an event management and marketing company that primarily assists nonprofit organizations. This is his story.

I've worked for this agency for about a year. However, I previously worked with a foundation for about four years. We manage and execute events for nonprofits. They might have charity fund-raiser dinners, golf tournaments, and so on. The charities we work for help children, veterans, and people with health problems. We will also help cities do food festivals and other events. I love what I do. I have more fun working with the corporations than with the charities. I love the events and the thrill of chasing sales.

At a recent golf event, we charged around $10,000 per foursome, had 200 people attend as well as various celebrities. This was followed by a silent and a live auction. We aim for netting 80 percent of the funds raised to go to the actual charity and only 20 percent to overhead. Sometimes this slips to 30 percent overhead. In the recent golf event, we netted $115,000, and 30 percent went to overhead. The celebrities usually appear for free. We have to pay for travel, hotel, and food.

One of the big questions in these events is, Who is driving the ship? Is it the corporate sponsor, the charity, or us? Sometimes there are a lot of disagreements, and we get caught in the middle between the charity and the corporate sponsor. The corporate sponsors want to spend more for overhead so it "looks good." This usually results in a smaller net. The charities don't want to fly in the celebrities and sometimes can be a little too cheap.

A lot of nonprofits have great causes but are not savvy businesspeople. Some don't even know how to put a database together. It is not always easy working for nonprofits.

My agency is for-profit. We give expertise and overhead. We charge a flat fee, get 20 percent commissions of cash brought in, and 10 percent of in-kind contributions. In-kind contributions include donated alcohol, golf course usage, food, et cetera. We are very flexible on the percentages and usually give money back to the charity.

We try to have a minimum flat fee of $25,000. We might discount that to $15,000 for a "sexy" event that also raises our profile.

You get what you pay for. We manage the event from A to Z. We help find the celebrities and sponsors, field conference calls, set up databases, help in hiring, and manage the actual event.

I am a big believer in having both a flat fee and a commission. With incentive laden deals we all work harder, and sometimes it is the only way to motivate people. The flat fee covers us in case of disaster.

There is tremendous mismanagement in nonprofits. They need more of a business approach.

Do not send the $10.

In financial services broadly, the word commission has largely come to be replaced with the "service compensation." To some extent, referencing a fee versus a commission signals the type of account in the financial sector. This language also reflects a response to conflicting attitudes about paying for a special service that is designed to promote consumption/growth or a fee with the overall potential to cut into company profits. There are a number of themes in this chapter that illustrate the variability evident in these conflicting attitudes.

One of the most clear-cut of the patterns in this data is the pervasiveness of hierarchy in the commission structure in financial services. Within and across companies, the commission structure imposes a hierarchy that is designed to select on those employees most motivated by the "business approach." In other words, the structure of the commission system appears to do what it is intended to do, which is weed out those who do not excel at sales early in their careers and orient employees toward thinking in terms of behavioral statistics, particularly outcomes. However, there is some ambiguity when it comes to commission structures that are complicated for new employees. If it is in fact the case as Norman states that "no one really understands" the commission system set up for new employees, it cannot possibly function as an incentive; although it may function as a mechanism for weeding out those who are not persistent.

Several of the respondents described various aspects of their business in terms of percentages. They did not simply state their cut. Many provided percentages regarding their individual sales, profitability, success rates, sales ratios, and even their own likability. It's unclear whether these are estimates or if their responses are based on behavioral statistics.

Another interesting theme worth mentioning is the number of respondents who refused payment for their participation. It may be impossible to tell why such a large number of the respondents refused payment for their participation. It is unlikely that $10 was not enough money because respondents who consider their time to be worth more than that would have refused participation. The response rate in this study was relatively high, and there were no apparent differences between job categories. There were no transaction costs associated with receiving payment, so it is unlikely that the economic value played a role in these decisions. It is possible that these decisions resulted from a desire to manage perceptions. In other words, people who were just talking about how much money they make may not want to accept $10 for ten to fifteen minutes of their time if they are concerned that they might come across as greedy or needy.[4] Alternatively, some people may simply think that it is not necessary because they consider their time an investment in something valuable (in knowledge perhaps) or that they did not do anything to "earn" the money. Another possible explanation arises from behavioral economics which might posit that respondents would give up the $10 simply because they would feel good about themselves (being altruistic). We can't presume to know what people think, but a better understanding of how individuals conceive of earning and what people value may reveal a great deal about the minimum economic incentive and the tipping point for economic motivation. The other fascinating point about the high rate of refusal for compensation of participants in financial services is that by comparison with other sectors one might expect those in financial services who are (at least in the popular conception) perceived to be motivated by greed to be the least likely to refuse money in any circumstance. Are they in fact less greedy, more concerned with the perception of others, or is this just a spurious finding?

There are some interesting incongruities or dilemmas of note in these narratives. For example, Richard stated that he liked his job because he likes helping people. He also noted that he makes most of his money on the commissions incurred when people pay points on a loan and that most of his customers are people who are poor. The curious puzzle of credit and commissions is that the commission structure is (at least in some cases) motivating some people to extend credit to people who are more likely to have to pay more for their loan and perhaps less likely to be able to afford it. Some of the narratives also hinted at a few of the ways in which credit markets are segregated. When Matthew mentioned that he uses lists of potential clients that have been "scrubbed" to reflect the legal restrictions on telemarketing, income, price, type of home and location, and the demographic characteristics of the clients that the company intends to pursue, a number of important questions arise. How do companies determine the characteristics that are likely to be most profitable to them? Do the characteristics that companies consider most profitable produce significant, sustainable growth? How does the commission structure vary in relationship to the consumers targeted by the various types of companies? Future research may explore how the micro and macro puzzles of credit impact economic growth. So, is greed good? Perhaps the more important question is, "Good for whom?"

NOTES

1. Elton, Gruber, Das, and Hlavka (1993) is an example of some of the research on fund performance and expenses. However, even this study looks at commissions broadly as an expense, not at the commission system specifically.

2. These terms are defined by Sean and Richard in the subsequent essays.

3. Term–life insurance is set at a fixed rate for a limited period of time. Whole insurance lasts for the lifetime of the person and also has an investment component which the person can borrow against.

4. This is not to imply that such is the perception, only that an individual respondent might be motivated by how she or he is perceived by others.

3

Realty

The Bureau of the Census reported that in 2008 there were 576,000 realtors in the United States with average annual earnings of $47,000. However, it should be noted that since the recession not only have real estate transactions declined, but the common percentages for real estate commissions have also gone down from 6 to 7 percent to 4 to 5 percent. In addition, it is also likely that the agencies are taking a bigger cut or allowing for a smaller cut to the realtor because sales have declined.

Realtor commissions are fees paid at the close of a real estate transaction to the listing agent and selling agent (although the two may be one in the same). Real estate commissions are usually split between the agent for the buyer and the agent for the seller. The commission can vary by contract, agency, and market region. Real estate agents are legally required to sign with a broker's agency. Agencies also reduce overhead for agents and brokers by providing or sharing the cost of advertising, marketing, office space and supplies, and so forth. The relationship between the agent/broker and agency results in the real estate agency or "house" receiving a cut of the commission. The commission structure between the agency and agent can be 50/50, 60/40, 70/30, or 80/20, depending on the experience and value that the agent brings to the agency and his or her skill in negotiating the contract.

If an agent splits a $15,000 commission with another agent, how much of the $7,500 does the agent keep? How much goes to pay for costs as well as to the company the agent is working for? Does the commission structure affect work effort or service quality? How competitive is the industry?

Most of us are aware that realtors typically make a commission of around 6 percent on the sale of a home or condominium. With the average nationwide sale price of an existing home at $244,000, a commission of almost $15,000[1] would appear to be easy money. In Washington, D.C., for example, the median price of an existing home was $520,000 in 2008 and over $1,000,000 in three zip codes. Given the earning potential in realty commissions, it is no surprise that there is intense competition. In a *Washington Post* article, Sandra Fleishman (2005) reported that in 2004 there were more than 2.5 million licensed realtors in the United States and that although many realtors in the Washington area did exceptionally well, other realtors were not financially successful.

For example, the commission structure on a house selling for $300,000 might resemble the following scenario. A 5 percent commission ($15,000) split equally between two separate agents is $7,500 each. A new agent is likely to have a 50/50 split with an agency, meaning that the house cut is $3,750. The agency may also deduct advertising fees from the commission check. Average advertising costs for a house in that price range in most regions might be about $350 per month. A house that took six months to sell may cost an agent $2,100 in advertising deductions. The agent's commission on this sale is actually $1,650. Consider a 40-hour workweek over 24 weeks. The result may be about $1.72 per hour before taxes! Deductions from the commission check after the initial house cut vary considerably, but even if there are no additional deductions, a new agent is still making approximately $3.91 per hour before taxes on this sale at best. It's unlikely that an agent would spend 40 hours per week for 24 weeks on a single house, but this means that agents rely at least somewhat on volume sales to increase the value of their time and value to the agency (which also affects their earning potential). In a 40-hour workweek, a realtor may have to work on an average of at least five homes worth approximately $300,000 each to make minimum wage.

This chapter examines the typical commission in real estate sales, the various commission structures, and the perspectives of realtors on the commission system. The chapter is organized in accordance with differences in the commission structures for real estate sales, rental properties, and real estate advertising. In addition, realtors explain competition within the industry. This chapter also provides a unique perspective on the commission system by exploring the experiences of realtors in various contexts and under different commission structures. These narratives offer an understanding of the motivation of realtors that may help identify how manipulating incentives might stimulate growth in the housing sector.

REAL ESTATE SALES

Commissions are paid to realtors upon the successful completion of a real estate transaction. However, what many people may not know is that clients have the right to negotiate real estate commissions. Increasing competition driven by new technologies and tighter markets coupled with the reduced demand from customers as more and more people sell their own homes or use realtor services à-la-carte have resulted in changes to what has been considered the standard commission in real estate sales. These days, there are discount brokers offering their services on commissions as low as 2 percent; although some brokers charge as much as 10 percent. The industry standard has been 5 to 6 percent, with some variation across the country. One of the most important functions that realtors often contend is crucial to selling properties quickly is the advertisement of properties, and new technologies have diffused the influence of the profession as people are now free to advertise and search for properties on websites like www.trulia.com, www.zillow.com, www.ForSaleByOwner .com, et cetera. However, people who sell their own homes have to confirm the pre-approval of potential buyers, complete state-specific real estate forms and contracts, work with the title company, and may have to hire a real estate attorney. These services are likely valuable to many people who do not have the time, knowledge, or desire to sell their own home, and while the standard 6 percent may seem like a lot of money, this does not necessarily reflect the profit that an individual realtor actually makes from the deal.

Susan works for a large realtor in Washington, D.C. She specifically asked that her real name not be used because the company has told employees they could not talk about commissions. This is her story.

In a typical house sale, a certain percentage goes to the seller's agent, and the remainder goes to the buyer's agent. The usual commission is 5 to 6 percent and is now more often 5 percent.[2] The split is not always even. It might be 2 to 3 percent and that amount would be known to the agent showing the house from the MLS.[3]

If our percent is 3 percent, the realtor company gets 20 percent, and I keep 80 percent. New agents might only get 50 to 60 percent. The more you sell, the better percentage you get (it goes up incrementally). It is hard on new agents. They sell less, and they get a lower percentage.

The realty company pays for some expenses. They will pay for ads in the major paper but not in the neighborhood paper. They will pay to produce the fact sheets, but I have to pay for the postage.

The split (80 percent/20 percent) is not affected by any costs. If the sale is kept in-house, I get to keep 85 percent instead of 80 percent.

If someone shows the house for me on a Sunday because I have two listings, the person doing the showing receives nothing from me. If someone walks in without an agent, then she will get the buyer's agent percentage. The person standing in for me also gets contacts and exposure.

If I am working for someone buying a house, the percentage works the same. I keep 80 percent and 20 percent goes to the realty company. I pay for some of the advertising that drums up business. I have an agreement with the realty company on what they will pay. I'm supposed to pay for advertising myself because I am technically an independent contractor. However, because I am senior, they will pay for some of the advertising and other expenses.

Martha has been selling houses in Washington, D.C., for over thirty years. The following narrative details her experiences with real estate commissions.

Our firm tries to get sellers to agree to 7 percent commissions. However, the reality is that most commissions are 5 percent or 6 percent. The agent negotiates with the seller, and it depends upon the competition. It is up to the agent to decide upon the commission percent. If the percentage is less than 5 percent, the agent must give more to the realty company.

The agent-realty split can really vary. For most new agents, it is 50 percent to the agent and 50 percent to the realty company. More senior agents will get 65 percent or so.

Some agencies somewhat resent the senior agents because of their higher split.

In some situations, the agents will get 90 to 100 percent. However, they pay a monthly desk fee instead. The monthly desk fee is about $1,500 a month.

The agent also pays $225 per transaction to the agency which I call a junk fee but the agency calls a "transaction cost." Some agents will try to pass this on to the seller.

The company pays for advertisements for selling the house. This is usually limited to five ads in the newspaper. After five ads, the agent may have to kick in some of the advertising costs. The company pays for most of the postage for mailing materials while the agent pays for printing.

I pay for my own advertising that drums up business. If a charity or school event in which I place an advertisement is sponsoring a charity race, I pay for it. The realty company does not kick in to this amount. This may be different at other companies. I am proud of our charitable activities in the community. The community has been good to us, and we try to be good to the community.

If the agent is representing the buyer, the same percentage breakdown occurs between agent and realty company.

If another agent is covering that day, there is no compensation. The other agent does this to meet potential buyers and sellers. It is a form of free advertising.

Agents are legally independent contractors. They market themselves. When agents send out general advertising, they pay for this advertising. Most companies have rules on how this is done. Most agents are really "lone gunners." However, there are some agents who work with teams. They have their own internal splits and might pay a salary to an administrative assistant.

Barbara has been a realtor in Newton, Massachusetts, for the past ten years. She likes her job and shared the following story about her experience with commissions.

The problem with commissions is that you don't make any money unless the property sells. That can take a long time. It can get very competitive with other realtors. Within our office, we all get along and help each other. We trust each other.

The typical commission in this area is 5 percent. In some situations, we might go for 4.5 percent. This is split down the middle with the seller's agent and the buyer's agent. If the house sells for $400,000, $10,000 goes to the buyer's agent and $10,000 to the seller's agent. If I am selling the house, 8 percent of the $10,000 ($800) will go to the national headquarters of the company. The remaining $9,200 ($10,000 minus $800) will be split between me and the local agency. When I started, I used to get 50 percent. Now I get 60 percent. More experienced agents get a higher percentage. So for this example, I would get 60 percent of $9,200 ($5,520).

The local headquarters pays for most of the advertising and things like my voicemail and office space. I pay for dues to the Multiple Listing Service, my realtor license, mailings to drum up business, and business cards. Sometimes if a special brochure has to be printed up, we negotiate over who will pay for it.

If someone is showing the house for you because you have two showings in one day or are on vacation and the house sells, they get $500. If I am on vacation for a week and they shepherd the sale through inspections and closings, that person would get 20 percent of my $5,520.

If I am working for a buyer, the same percentages apply. I would get 60 percent of the split given to my side. There are situations where the total commission is 4 percent instead of 5 percent. In those situations, I might have a stipulation in my contract with the buyer. That stipulation is that the buyer would make up the difference, so I would still get half of 5 percent (2.5 percent).

If I am selling a house and a buyer comes in without an agent, it can be a little stressful. It becomes a little unclear whom you are working for. In those situations, the contract might call for a 4 percent commission. All sides would benefit. I would be called a facilitator.

Jack is a realtor in a Colorado resort town. He is discussed in the companion volume on tipping for his work as a ski instructor. This is what Dave had to say about commissions in real estate.

I mostly sell houses and condos. We don't do rentals. The average commission is 6 percent, which is usually split equally between the seller's agent and buyer's agent. There is some negotiation here. The parent company (Century 21) gets 8 percent off the top, and then the remaining of the 3 percent is split 50/50 between me and the realty company. If I have over a million dollars in sales, my percentage would be 55 percent. The condo market is good with condos selling for $250,000 plus.

The office pays for advertising. Because I am new, a lot of my business depends on referrals. If someone refers someone to me, they get 25 percent of my bottom line. If a broker refers someone to our office, our office will give the other broker 25 to 35 percent of the bottom line. In essence, if I know the person who made the referral, I pay that person a referral fee, and the office pays if the referral came from another broker. A broker cannot pay an individual for a referral.

We don't have a lot of competition in the office. We are a small office. We try to have a good time. A few weeks ago, I took someone else's client out for a day to look at property, and I got $500 just for showing them around. It was very easy money. They did buy something. If someone sells something of mine while I am on vacation, I will split it 50/50. We are very low key.

Tom owns a realty company in Florida that employs ten independent contractors. This is his story.

The typical commission is 6 to 7 percent. We are at the lower end. Our houses sell for $150,000 to $200,000. Like other realty companies, the commissions are split evenly between the buyer and seller agents. If a house sells for $200,000 at a 6 percent commission, our cut is 3 percent or $6,000. The agent keeps 50 percent. Agents who sell more can keep 60 percent and in some situations 70 percent. There is a sliding scale.

We do all the institutional advertising. If the agent does a flyer at a church, he might pay for that. I provide the first set of business cards for new agents, and they buy cards after that. I will pay the postage for mass mailings, and they will pay for paper.

The same percentage breakdown with the agent occurs whether you are buying or selling the house. If we represent both sides, we lower the commission by usually half a percentage point.

We try to limit the competition among the agents. We started out as a family business, and we try to work together. A lot of other agencies fight a lot. I tell new agents if they want to get rich they have to first learn how to do service. It requires cooperation. If you get mad at another agency, you can't lock them out when looking at properties. It only hurts you in the long run. You have to get along.

Monique sold new homes for a developer for six months in the Washington, D.C., area. The following narrative details her experience with commissions in real estate.

I like my job. However, the company was not well-organized. It was owned by a bunch of college buddies, and there was a lot that was unfair. Our sales manager put too much time into selling, so he could make his own commissions. A lot was determined by whim. If he liked you, you could do well. If you were on his bad side—watch out.

I had a base salary of $20,000 a year. I received 1 percent commission at settlement. The houses ranged from $500,000 to $900,000. Often, by the time the extras were computed, the house would sell for $1 million. I sold five houses in six months.

We worked out of a trailer because the model home was not yet ready. A lot of people would stop by, and we also did a lot of outreach. Realtors who brought people to view the homes received 3 percent commissions. Ninety-five percent of customers had a realtor. We would give the realtors more than the 3 percent. They would get $1,000 extra for their first home, $2,500 for their second home, and $3,500 for each additional home. We also sent out postcards to the local community and used other sales techniques.

It was difficult surviving on the $20,000 base pay. Usually, construction would not begin for 6 months after signing, and it took at least 6 months to build the home. I had to wait 6 to 18 months after signing until I got my 1 percent. If you could hold out with the base pay, you could do OK in this job.

Within my division I was the only salesperson, so there was not much competition. However, I sometimes sent a person to a less expensive area where they had a model home. The salesperson in that area would try to sell the person a home in that area. I lost houses that way. Another agent lost a sale when a minor modification to the sale occurred and another salesperson took credit and got the $8,000. There was a lot of bad blood. It really is too cutthroat, and that is one reason why I left.

Another problem with the job is that I had to work every Saturday and Sunday.

Customers put down 5 percent deposits, and it was up to the sales manager if they got the deposit back if they cancelled. Some people put down more than 5 percent because they wanted to reduce the final mortgage. About half the sales did not go through after closing.[4] Often the person could not get financing. If they could not get financing, they got their deposit back.

Please don't send the $10. I am happy to help out.

Samantha has worked for the last two years as a leasing consultant in northern Virginia. This is what she had to say about commissions.

We manage 851 apartments. I get people to lease them. I love my job. I fell into this job. I got my degree in communications, and I thought I would go to law school. However, I use my communication skills every day, and I interact with a lot of different people.

I get paid $19 an hour. Part of my salary is based upon the fact that I also supervise. People who don't supervise get $12 to $14 an hour.

My commission is based on two factors. If I lease 3 apartments per month, I get $50 per unit. For 4 to 5 units, I get $75 per unit, and for 6 or more units, I get $100 per unit. Last month, I rented 10 apartments and got $800 in commissions. This is pretty typical for me.

We also get a bonus each quarter. The bonus is complicated to compute but is based on our retention level, occupancy rate, and several other factors. Last quarter we got $800 per person in the office.

Martha has worked for a realtor in the San Francisco area for four years. This is her story.

I love my work. I'm my own businessperson. I can make as much money as I want if I work hard.

The typical percentage for the sale of a house is 6 percent. This is usually split equally between the buyer's and seller's agent. However, sometimes in order to get the listing, the seller's agent will agree to take 2 percent and sell the house for a 5 percent commission (3 percent going to the buyer's agent).

For a house selling for a million dollars, the typical 6 percent commission would have each side making $30,000. I personally get 50 percent of that after expenses. My expenses include advertising, errors and omissions insurance,[5] realtor fees, MLS listing, and other marketing materials. These costs usually add up to $6,000 to $7,000 per year. When I sell more houses, I get a higher percentage. After my sales have resulted in $20,000 in commission for the realty company in a given year, I start getting 100 percent of the commission in my subsequent sales (I still pay for expenses). Twenty thousand dollars in commissions translates into $2 million in sales (about four transactions).

The same percentages work if I am working for a buyer.

I also sell mobile homes. The typical commission for mobile homes is 8 to 10 percent instead of the typical 6 percent. However, the splits work in the same way. Mobile home sales are slow. The ones I sell go mostly to senior citizens who want to live in retirement-type communities.

She refused to take the $10 for her participation. She requested that the money be donated to an AIDS support group, which was done in her name.

Newbell has been a real estate agent in Ohio for the past two years. Most of the properties he sells are in blighted neighborhoods. Newbell had this to say about commissions.

I like my job. I interact with a lot of people, and I help people make the most important financial decision of their lives. However, the money does not always come in every month.

I work for a company that has twenty agents. Our commission is about 7 percent. Many of our houses are small and are listed for under $100,000. Our minimum commission is $2,500. We always split the commission down the middle. This makes it easy.

We try to have our firm represent both the buyer and the seller. We give them a disclosure agreement and have different agents represent each side.

If I sell a $500,000 house, the commission is 7 percent ($35,000). If we represent both the seller and the broker, the firm would get half of this and each of the agents would get 25 percent. If the buyer has a realtor from another firm, our firm gets half of the commission, and I would get half of that. I would still get 25 percent.

The owner of our company pays for all advertising and the MLS listing. I pay for only a few small items that I work out with the buyer or seller such as a termite inspection. This is usually under $100.

There is a lot of competition. Some agents are at the throats of other agents 24-7. They try to take other deals. Someone will call about a property listed with another agent, and they will say, "I can help you." There are twenty hungry agents. It can get real ugly with slamming of doors. A person can lose $3,000 to $4,000. The owner tries to give everyone equal floor time for when people walk in.

You have to be there when people call. Two ladies were fired last year for stealing deals.

You need to be clear with the client. People have convenient amnesia. They will try to give you 2.5 percent instead of 7 percent. You have to be stern.

Francis has been a realtor in San Francisco for eight years and shared the following story.

I love it. I have my own schedule, and I don't have to work with people that I don't like. I sell condos and homes. We don't do rentals.

The typical commission used to be 6 percent, but it is moving toward 5 percent with a softer real estate market. The prices are so high that 5 percent is still a lot of money.

For a million dollar "starter home" in San Francisco, the commission is 5 percent or $50,000. Half would go to the buyer's agent and half to the seller's agent. So if I was representing the seller, we would get $25,000. Eight percent of that $25,000 ($2,000) is given to the national office for advertising and to the local office for overhead. Of the remaining $23,000, I get 70 percent, and the remainder goes to the real estate company.

Newer agents start at 60 percent. If they make more than $34,700 a year in commission, they then start getting 70 percent. They could also be downgraded back to 60 percent. They are re-evaluated each year.

The company will pay for one advertisement per week in the local paper for three months. After that they make you reduce the price. However, the ad has a limited number of lines and puts the company phone number on the ad rather than yours. That means that the "floor person" at the realty company often gets the call. Hence, most of us pay for our own ads which can be larger and have our own phone numbers. This costs me $75 a week. I also pay for brochures. They pay for the sign in front of the house, but I pay for the rider which has my name and number on it. We pay for the signs that are displayed on the days the house is shown (about $250) and for errors and omissions insurance ($1,500 a year). Some managers will give some of these start-up costs (the signs and cost of training) back to the agent after the first sale.

The same percentage structure works if I am a buyer's agent. It very rarely occurs that I represent both the buyer and the seller. Although a dual agency is legal, I still feel I would have a conflict of interest. In these cases, we would get another agent in my office to serve as the other agent.

Most buyers expect a present at the end of the deal. I usually give a present in the $400-$500 range. That could be a washer or dryer. Some clients expect as much as an $800 present. There are a lot of under-the-table kickbacks. I don't do them. There is a cultural component. Koreans expect it. Some agents give money back. We are not allowed to do that in our office, and I don't do it.

We have some squabbles among the agents, but stealing clients is not done in my office. One agent took a troublesome client of mine by mistake, and he felt really bad about it. We talked about it.

At another agency where I worked, there were wars and a lot of shenanigans. Agents would interfere with each other. It was a very competitive office, and people were not very nice. The problem was really a managerial problem. I left because of the squabbles.

Francis would not take the $10 for participating in the interview and said give it to a charity. The $10 participation payment was donated to the homeless in Washington, D.C.

There are a few themes evident in these narratives. Many of those in real estate shared stories of their current employment and compared some of those experiences with similar work in other agencies. Those responses indicate that highly competitive work environments may lead some employees who seem to be motivated by customer service to seek employment in a more cooperative work environment. Also, those respondents tended to report liking the work on the whole; while the work environment did not seem to negatively impact their job satisfaction, it did appear to affect their decisions to work in another agency.

These stories also lend support to the notion that consistency is an important factor in the assessment of managerial efficacy and the perception of fairness in the commission system. Although many in real estate are at the mercy of market forces, most report that they like their work. In particular, a number of the respondents in realty reported that the primary reason that they were satisfied with their work was due to the extent to which their pay reflects work effort.

The realty professionals interviewed understood the commission structure that they worked within very well, and the commissions obviously affected their actions and behavior at work. However, a number of respondents also appeared to be motivated by helping people with an important life decision like buying a home. Some appeared to have a commitment to competency and integrity that was independent of their individual economic concerns. For example, Francis in San Francisco stated that she would not represent both sides in a sale (even though it is legal and common practice) because she felt that she would inevitably have a conflict of interest. She indicated that in those cases she would pull another agent from the agency to assist the other party. The economic cost to Francis may also be considered an investment in a cooperative work environment.

RENTAL PROPERTIES

Commissions on rental properties may be paid by the landlord or the tenant and are most often referred to as a fee. Responsibility for paying the fee and the amount of the fee or commission are generally negotiated in advance between the owner and broker. The standards tend to vary by city or county and are generally a function of local market conditions. A finder's fee or retainer paid by a tenant is more likely when the demand for rental properties is high, and the commission is more likely to be paid by the landlord or subsidized by the landlord when an owner wants to attract renters or particular types of renters in a competitive market.

Barbara has been a realtor in Newton, Massachusetts, for the past ten years. Although she likes her job, she tends to avoid property rentals because she does not perceive it to be the best use of her time. During her interview, she spoke about real estate sales (included in the previous section) and property rentals. The following details her responses regarding commissions on property rentals.

We also make commissions with apartment rentals. I don't do too many of these. Typically, the commission is one month's rent—say $2,000. This would be split within our office as 80 percent to me and 20 percent to the office. When it was a hot market, this was paid by the renter. With the market for rental units cooling, this is now sometimes split by the landlord and the renter. In some situations, the landlord will pick up the full $2,000 in order to induce a rental.

A landlord can simultaneously use many different realty companies. Each realtor would advertise, and each pay for the advertising.

Tom owns a realty company in Florida that employs ten independent contractors. Tom describes rentals as a hassle but potentially lucrative, particularly as many renters buy eventually. His responses regarding real estate sales are included in the previous section, and the following responses are specific to rental properties.

We also do rentals. We take 10 percent of the rents. The agent gets half of the first month, and the rest stays in the office. We manage the property, so we get 10 percent each month, and repairs are deducted from the proceeds. Rentals are a hassle but can be lucrative. When sales are slow, it really can help out. Nevertheless, collections and other issues can be a problem. We pay for the advertisements for the rentals. A lot of people who end up buying homes start as renters. Rentals help the firm bring in money as well as meet potential new clients for buying properties.

Martha has worked for a realtor in the San Francisco area for four years. She likes her job but does not like brokering rentals because they are a hassle relative to the time they consume in her estimation. In the section on real estate sales, Martha reveals that she sells a diverse range of properties, but the following represent her responses that are specific to commissions on rental properties.

I also do rentals. This is not by choice. Rentals are a hassle and do not pay well. I typically get 25 percent of the first month's rent. So, for a $2,000-a-month rental I would get $500. I also pay for the cost of advertising (typically around $100). One of the problems is that there is a very soft rental market. Once, I got 4 percent of the first year's rent. This is because the condo had been on the market a long time.

Newbell has been a real estate agent in Ohio for the past two years. He too likes his job but hates dealing with rental properties. Newbell discussed real estate sales commissions in the previous section. This is what he had to say regarding rental property commissions.

We do rentals. I hate them. I won't do them anymore. My first rental had me taking 5 percent every month for the rental. It went really badly. It lasted three months until she stopped paying. The thing to do is to take the first full month's rent.

Realtors who provide rental services and those who do not offer rental services tend to agree that the commission on rentals is not commensurate with the time that they spend on the property. Among realtors who provide rental services, they either do it because they are required by their agency to provide the service and/or because they hope that rental customers might eventually procure their services to buy or sell a property. In addition, because rental properties are not usually listed with an exclusive agent, the commission structure does not incentivize work effort, and the fact that agents may have to spend time enforcing the contract further undermines the system. There are two possible barriers to optimizing rental markets suggested by these narratives. First, the structure of commissions does not adequately incentivize moving rental properties. Second, good faith in contracting in the rental market is not as credibly signaled and imposes greater enforcement costs than in real estate sales.

REAL ESTATE ADVERTISING

Marketing real estate has evolved from brochures and direct mailings to call capture technology in which a potential buyer can call an agent's 800 number listed on a for sale sign that provides a brief audio tour and generates an automatic lead for the agent. Some agents do their own advertising, some work for agencies that assist with advertising, and some outsource marketing. This is one case in which new technologies have been more of a benefit to the commission-based sales force. There are several ways in which new technologies are being employed, allowing agents to cut costs, save time, and network efficiently. Products like DocuSign and eFax allow agents to conduct paperless business in a highly efficient and cost-effective manner. Virtual meeting products, e-mail, and social networking sites are also among the tools used to market real estate more efficiently. These technologies have also meant that those who embrace them faster gain a competitive advantage.

Advertising real estate was once a potential entrée into real estate sales. However, more technical marketing campaigns are more often being handled by individual agents cutting costs or by corporate advertising firms who specialize in technological and marketing innovations. We did not have the opportunity to interview many people who make commissions marketing real estate, but the following narrative illustrates how commissions for real estate advertisements operate.

Betty worked in real estate advertising in Maryland. The following narrative reflects her experience receiving commissions.

I like what I do. My mom is a realtor, and I would like to be a realtor some day. I would be very good at it.

I designed the postcards that are sent out by realtors to drum up business. It would take a couple of hours to do the design. I get paid $50 for the initial design. If any listings resulted from the postcard, I would get an additional $100. If an actual rental occurred, I would get another $50, and for a sale, I could get up to $500.

I also designed door hangers which had the same pricing structure.

I also made money by helping send e-mails to people in the neighborhood when a new listing was available. I got paid $50, but I would not get a commission. I don't know how they got the e-mails.

I also helped make phone calls to past clients and people who had visited other listings. If the number of calls was small, I would do them for free. If I made over fifty calls, I would charge $10 or $20. It went very quickly, and there were few people who hung up on me.

NOTES

1. $244,000 x .06 = $14,640.

2. On how the traditional 6 percent commission rate is being eroded by the Internet and other market forces, see: Damon Darlin, "The Last Stand of the 6-Percenters?" *New York Times*, September 3, 2006.

3. Most realtors list houses and condos they are selling on the Multiple Listing Service (MLS). This allows others to search for available housing.

4. Cancellations of home sales, both new and older homes, have been rising given the "downturn" in the housing market. See: June Fletcher and Ruth Simon, "The New Word in Home Sales: 'Canceled,'" *Wall Street Journal*, November 3, 2006, W1.

5. Errors and omissions insurance protect professions such as attorneys, realtors, and insurance agents against liability suits in case of any potential error they may have made.

4

Agents

In popular culture, agents "show me the money." This chapter explores the work of agents who find and negotiate employment for the person they are representing or are intermediaries when the person is trying to sell a product or service. The Census Bureau reports that there were 33,000 agents and business managers who represented artists, performers, and athletes in 2008. Their average annual earnings at that time were estimated at around $51,000. The cut for agents representing the work of others depends not only on the commission structure but on their ability to attract and retain the highest yielding clients.

Agent representation of employment is intended to minimize transaction costs by making efficient connections between job opportunities and qualified candidates, minimizing information asymmetries, and acting as an intermediary to ensure the interests align effectively to minimize the problems of moral hazard and adverse selection. Agents are also expected to be skilled in negotiation so as to optimize contracts (that are ideally mutually beneficial). Agents procure and negotiate contracts for the clients that they represent. The clients may be a potential employee or an employer. Agents work in search firms. They might be independent talent scouts. They may work in large publishing houses. Business agents who seek highly-skilled executives or professionals to meet the needs of a corporate client might be called "headhunters." Agents who represent the work of others specialize in a profession, such as sports, business, temporary employment, publications, entertainment, and so on.

Sports agents, for example, procure and negotiate contracts between players and the various sports franchises. However, they have responsibilities that

47

go far beyond employment contracts. Sports agents represent players in endorsement deals in which agents are expected to secure additional income for athletes by finding products for the players to promote. This requires athletes to develop and maintain a popular reputation, and the agent's role is in handling public relations matters to develop, maintain, and protect the reputation those endorsements are based upon. Some agents in large firms also manage other aspects of the athlete's finances, including taxes and investments. Often, agents begin recruiting clients in their teenage years and provide a great deal of personal and professional guidance throughout the athlete's career. Many agents have some background in law that gives them an advantage in developing reliable contracts in which there are inherently complex legal matters involved. For all this work, sports agents typically get a commission of about 4 to 5 percent on each contract.

Literary agents, for example, represent writers. They act as an intermediary or "gatekeeper," developing their own reputations by presenting high-quality, profitable written works to publishers, theatrical producers, and film producers. Literary agents most often negotiate contracts for novelists, screenwriters, and writers of commercial works of nonfiction. The work of literary agents is intended to moderate the connections between publishing houses and writers so as to maintain the credibility and value of commercial publications. Their work is crucial to managing the vast information asymmetries intrinsically related to modern publication contracts, which may involve multiple layers of complexity considering international marketing, media regulations, variations in professional standards and practices, and so forth. The literary agent also acts as a mediator so that the business and creative elements of the contract are most efficiently and effectively handled. Literary agents may operate their own agencies or work in large firms, but most agencies tend to specialize to at least some degree. Legitimate agents are not required to be members of the Association of Authors' Representatives (AAR), but most literary agents in the United States are members. And, an author seeking a lucrative publishing house would be ill advised to work with an agent who is not a member of AAR. Membership in AAR requires an agent to have already established a reputation by having sold a minimum number of books and to adhere to the professional code of ethics of the organization. An author may acquire the representation of a legitimate agent by submitting a query, which is essentially an unsolicited proposal for representation for a specific work. Legitimate literary agents do not charge reading fees, demand retainers, or bill for operating expenses. Agents representing authors derive their income from the 10 to 20 percent commission on the proceeds of sales made on the behalf of their client.

A headhunter, recruiter, business agent, or executive search agent engages in the solicitation of individuals to fill jobs within a firm. Similar to agents representing other types of work, recruiting agents are responsible for minimizing the transaction costs associated with turnover. Recruiters may work internally for one organization, or they may work for multiple clients in a third-party broker relationship. Internal recruiters may function in a general Human Resources (HR) capacity by negotiating and managing contracts, hiring professionals, firing employees, conducting exit interviews, managing employee disputes, and administrating benefits packages. Although, internal recruiters might instead have a more specific recruiting function either within HR or as a contracted employee or agency. Third-party recruiters or headhunters serve as an intermediary between the client companies and the candidates they recruit for certain types of positions. An executive search firm is a type of employment agency that specializes in hunting agency executives, and they typically have a particular expertise and set of personal contacts that positions them for this kind of specialized work. The commission structure for recruiters varies by category. Contingent recruiters may earn 10 to 35 percent of the first year base salary or total remuneration as a hiring fee. Retained recruiters tend to make commissions of smaller percentages but have more stable income.

A temporary staffing agent does a job similar to that of the recruiter. However, the contingent nature of the work that employment agencies staff makes for significant differences in the job obligations and compensation. A temporary staffing agent matches workers to open jobs. Often, these jobs are provisional, or certain aspects of these jobs result in high turnover for the firm utilizing the employment agency. Employment agencies in this category may also hire for permanent positions, in which case the agency might make up to 20 percent of the candidate's salary upon completion of the probationary period. The staffing agent will then get a cut of that percentage based on his or her own contract with the employment agency. When employment agencies fill temporary positions, the agency gets a percentage of the candidate's compensation based on the hours worked and the contract negotiated between the client (the company receiving assistance to fill a position) and employment agency. The individual staffing agent's commission is a percentage of this contracted cut in accordance with the agent's own contract. There is undoubtedly a great deal of variation and complexity in the commission system designed to manage unemployment.

Taylor has worked for a temp agency in Washington, D.C., for the past six years and shared the following story about commissions.

I love my work. It is a great working environment. I get to wear shorts, and it is fun. We mostly provide temps for law firms—paralegals, receptionists, and so on. There are two types of positions that we fill: permanent positions and regular temping.

For permanent positions, the client pays us 20 percent of their salary and the account representative gets 40 percent of that. Therefore, if the position was for $100,000, our firm would get $20,000, and the account rep would get $8,000. The law firm (client) pays for this.

We also do regular temping. A firm might hire several temps. The account rep receives his commission according to hours worked. If a firm has 5,000 hours for a month (several temps), the account rep gets paid for 15 percent of the 5,000 hours, or 750 hours. Our firm makes money by charging a 50 percent markup. If a receptionist gets $10 an hour, we will charge the client $15 an hour.

We have two people that do regular temping. They get salary plus commissions. The salaries are in the $60,000 to $80,000 range. We have eight people who do permanent positions, and they receive straight commission.

Applicants submit resumes to us. We clean them up, check on their references, and do all the legwork. Our firm has been in business for thirty years, so 90 percent of our business comes from old clients. We also do a lot of cold calls. We look at *Legal Times*, the phone book, online, and so on. We first make sure that they are not already a client. I make about fifty of these calls a week. Maybe 1 percent ends up with some business.

The hardest part is finding new clients (not new job seekers). Clients do not want to pay our fee. We have some that negotiate temp to permanent positions so that after 500 hours they no longer have to pay. However, they will pay a higher rate up front.

Please don't send money.

Charles has worked for the last two years at an executive search firm in New York City. This is his story.

I like what I do. I get to interact with a variety of people. The searches are different from one another, and they are interesting. We mostly do recruitment in the real estate industry. This might be for developers or for finance firms, and so on. The positions we look for are $200,000 a year and up.

We first meet with the potential clients and pitch our business. We demand an exclusive retainer. If the position is filled in any way, we still get paid. The industry standard is that we receive 33 percent of the first year's salary. We might get 30 percent if the firm has several searches with us.

We get three separate retainers. If the position is for $250,000, we will eventually receive $82,500. We get three retainers of $20,000 each and the remainder when the position is filled. The client can cancel within sixty days and get most of their money back. We fill 95 percent of the searches we start. On average, it takes ninety days to fill a position, and I am presently working on eight positions.

Our expenses are pretty minimal. We don't usually advertise. The client pays for travel. We pay for video conferencing and other related expenses. To fill a position, we research the Internet, look at conference attendance lists, and use our database, connections, and referrals. We don't give referral fees.

My salary is $75,000 per year, and I received a $5,000 bonus at the end of the year. I do not get commission, and the source of my bonus is not quantifiable. My understanding is that the partners get half of the commission. Therefore, if the commission is $82,500, the partner would get $41,250, and the rest would go to the firm.

Nancy has been a headhunter in the Washington, D.C., area for fourteen years. This is what she had to say about commissions for recruiting.

Most days I love what I do. I have the lifestyle that I want. I can afford to put my kids through school. I have a flexible schedule, and I don't have to work very long hours. The job has a lot of variety but is not intellectually stimulating.

I specialize in placing professionals who have masters' degrees or PhDs into research positions. These research positions include health care policy, finance, survey statisticians, and so on.

My clients are the companies that are looking for positions to fill. I market to the companies and try to build relations. The companies only pay if someone is hired. The pay is usually based upon annual salary. Sometimes they also pay a percentage of bonuses or other commitments. Our firm usually gets 30 percent of the annual salary. There are some situations where we will take a retainer (usually a third) which we will keep in return for more work on our part and a lower overall commission (perhaps 20 percent).

We guarantee the person for thirty days. We find them, but we don't re-train them. However, I will work with the company and the person to get the position to work.

I earn 50 percent of the cash I bring into the business. I averaged $309,000 of business per year over the last five years. I get 50 percent of that. Because I am in the top 10 percent, I also qualify for company paid trips. I fill a dozen positions a year. My success rate is about 50 percent.

I market and do recruitment. I have a database that I have developed over the last seven to eight years. I find people through associations, networks, Internet research, articles, and our competitor Web sites. The average search takes two to four months. I prep candidates and do follow-up. In the average search, I talk to the client for several hours and talk to ten or more candidates. I might spend up to one hundred hours on a complicated search.

It is frustrating that I cannot go to the interviews. I can do all the setup or prep in the world, but the actual "sale" takes place between the professional and the company representative. It is probably 80 percent chemistry after all the required skills have been met. All I can do is set the stage.

It takes a lot to do my job right. We train ten to twenty people for one person who makes it. We are a franchise and have hundreds of offices worldwide.

Please don't send me the $10.

Peter was a literary agent for three years. The following narrative details his experience with commissions.

I liked working with authors. However, in order to make it work, I would have to live in New York City, and I did not want to do that.

I got 15 percent of whatever the authors received. The royalty check would come to me, and I would distribute it. I sometimes contacted authors, and I was also flooded with proposals. I received over eight hundred proposals in three years. I took twenty to twenty-five of them at any given time. I probably took a total of fifty over the three years.

I generally received a short proposal from most authors with a few chapters or more. If I was not grabbed in the first few pages, I would stop reading.

I knew a lot of the key people and editors. I contacted them and pitched the proposal with a short one- to two-page letter asking them for an invitation to send more. For those that were finally placed, it might take six to twelve contact attempts. If it was over twelve attempts, I knew there was a problem. I sold probably 40 percent of the fifty proposals that I took.

About half of the books I placed came with advances. I was mostly dealing with first-time authors or those who had small book sales in the past. The typical advance for one of these books was a couple thousand dollars.

The typical royalty for authors was 10 percent of the list price for trade books and 10 percent of the net for academic books.

Being a literary agent is an inside thing. Editors like to get proposals from other editors they knew in the past. It is a very incestuous process, and I needed to be in New York to make it work. The agent is a gatekeeper for the publisher.

The public perception of huge advances for book contracts is wrong for the vast majority of authors.

I am now an editor for a well-known small press. I have a salary of about $70,000. This is a fairly high salary because I have twenty years of experience.

I also get bonuses. The bonus is based upon two factors: how many books I signed and their expected acquisition. This year my goal is $2 million in signing. This is based upon sales forecasts.

My bonus is also based upon the books that were published this year and their sale amounts. My total bonus is capped at a possible $12,000. I made 100 percent of that last year. Most, if not all of the senior people get their bonus because the purpose is to retain staff. This is the industry standard.

Lamont is a music booking agent based in Chicago. He shared the following story about his commissions as a booking agent.

I book rock performers for shows. I like it very much because I enjoy music, and I like being involved in the lives of musicians.

I almost always get 10 percent of what the performer receives, but this fluctuates a bit. If I represented a very large group like the Rolling Stones, I would probably get 8 percent. We represent mid-size groups. They will receive from $250 up to $50,000 per show. It really varies. I only receive a percentage on performance. The group's manager would also receive a percentage on CD sales, T-shirts, and so on.

The agency I work for has seventy-five groups, and I represent sixteen of them. About half of the time I will solicit a group, and the other half they will solicit me. There are many small bands that will solicit me.

I do not have exclusive contracts with groups, although some agencies do. However, in my eight years, I have had only one group leave.

There are a standard set of venues that I would approach in D.C. Their seating capacity ranges from 600 to 1,200. For example, the Black Cat will seat 600 and the 9:30 Club will seat 1,200. Sometimes I contact the venues, and sometimes they contact me. In smaller towns it is more likely they will contact me. Often they have heard of the group via the grapevine, or they had a good experience with them in the past.

There are a variety of different models by which the bands get paid.

1. In some situations there is simply a guarantee, say $1,000.
2. Sometimes there is a guarantee plus bonus. The guarantee might be $1,000, and after a certain split point, we will share the profit or the door. Usually the performer would get 85 percent after all expenses (hotel rooms, promotion costs, etc.) are met. Sometimes it might be much less if the group will not generate liquor sales.
3. With the door deal, the performers would get a straight percentage of the gross. So if 500 tickets are sold at $10, the performers would usually get 60 percent ($3,000).

4. We might also have a flat vs. percentage where we would get whichever is highest.

No matter what model is used, we get 10 percent of what the artist receives. Usually there is a negotiation process back-and-forth with the venue. Amounts are usually paid after the show. However, we might get our percentage in advance from expected revenues. Sometimes the final payment comes from the artist and other times from the venue.

Kelly has been an agent for actors and actresses for thirteen years. The following narrative reflects her responses during the interview.

I like what I do. My medium is developing people. I see them at the start of their career, and I get to see them develop. I help people pursue their dreams. I have about 1,000 clients. I find work for my clients in commercials, movies, and TV shows. I find this work through making contacts with studios and establishing relationships with different casting services.

Under the rules of the Screen Actor's Guild and American Federation of Television and Radio Artists, I always get a 10 percent commission. Some actors also have managers who get between 5 percent and 15 percent commission. The managers deal with their personal lives and will also help them find work. It seems that most managers have around ten clients.

The minimum amount that the actors are paid is determined by union rules. I don't remember the exact amounts, but I believe the minimum is $535 for an eight-hour day as well as residuals. Residuals are paid for programs that are rebroadcast. The amount of the residual is determined by a fairly complex formula that takes into account the original contract, where the showing occurs (the Super Bowl pays a lot more than a show late at night), and other factors. This residual rate is pre-negotiated between SAG and the buyer of the show. SAG has books which detail these amounts.

Once an actor gets started, they usually do not use SAG rates. The actor has a "quote" which lists what they have been paid in the past and determines what their minimum amounts are for the future. Beyond the SAG minimums, the payment rate is negotiated. The amount my clients get ranges from $600 to $6,000 per day. For a typical TV series in which an actor has lines and appears in several of its shows, they can get as much as $20,000 to $30,000 per show. Obviously, for named actors, they will get much more. The amounts really vary.

Payments go to the talent agencies who cut me a check, and I in turn cut a check to the actor. Sometimes I get the check directly.

Please, don't send me $10.

Lance is a sports agent. His perspective on commissions for representing athletes is presented in the following narrative.

I represent five basketball players for the NBA. I negotiate their contract, and I help them with marketing. I've been doing this for five years, and I like it a lot. I love basketball. I enjoy talking to people, and I am a very competitive person in a very competitive business. You would not know the names of the five players I represent.

The NBA allows me to get up to 4 percent of a player's salary. In the NFL, the upper limit is 3 percent. The 4 percent in the NBA is negotiable. Some agents might only get 1 percent. I get 3 percent for each of my five players. I also get 20 percent from all marketing, which ranges from T-shirts to advertisements to appearances. This 20 percent is also negotiable; although 20 percent is the industry standard.

Some agents represent players in the European leagues. The typical commission in Europe is between 10 percent and 20 percent. However, in Europe, the teams pay and not the players. In Europe, you might also split the commission with a European agent.

There is a lot of competition among agents. There are 900 certified agents in the NBA and only 31 first-round draft picks. Over half the agents have no claims on players. I talk to the coaches, parents, and other players. It is all about relationships. I go to all the games.

I give a lot of individual service. I will help players get trainers and financial managers. I try to help them as much as possible. I don't charge extra for this.

The negotiations are fairly established. New players salaries are determined by their place in the draft, and free agents salaries are affected by their age and number of years they have played. Negotiations can take one day for some players and three weeks for others.

There are a lot of unscrupulous people in this business. Some agents hire professional models for players. Other agents help their parents buy a house while they are still amateurs, and others give money to the coaches under the table.

Wanda has been a sales rep for a large academic publishing house for about a year. This is her story in her own words.

I like my job a lot. I used to teach at a university, and I love books, learning; and I have a background in sales. This is a good blend for me.

Most reps in our company have base salaries between $35,000 and $40,000. We also have bonuses based upon annual goals. My goal for my region is $3.5 million. There are eight different regions. There is a different rep for Amazon.com and other wholesalers.

If I meet my goal, I get a bonus of $10,000 to $12,000. If I exceed my goal by 30 percent, I get an additional bonus of $30,000. About half the reps make their goals. The goals are being revised because it is difficult for some to reach their goals.

Please don't send me the $10 as I know how hard it is to get research monies.

The narratives in this chapter depict that tremendous variation in job obligations and compensation among those who represent the work of others. The commission structure is complex, variable, and tends to reward experience. It is also interesting to note the extent to which agents perceive their success to be linked to the art of developing relationships. There is not a lot of information about what this means, how it's done, or under what conditions the art is conveyed in a manner that produces results for the agent.

5

Direct Marketing

This chapter details the commission system and the experiences of those working in telemarketing and unsolicited sales. The relevant U.S. Census Bureau occupational categories for this chapter are door-to-door sales workers, news and street vendors, and related workers and telemarketers. There are an estimated 69,000 door-to-door sales and related workers in the United States making an average of $25,000 per year, and there are approximately 60,000 telemarketers making an average annual income of around $23,000.

Telemarketing is a method of direct marketing in which prospective customers are offered unsolicited products or services. This marketing technique is a pitch conducted over the phone or Internet to attempt to sell, generate sales leads, or schedule an appointment for a face-to-face sales pitch. Telemarketing is a specific type of direct marketing, but both door-to-door sales and telemarketing are generally unsolicited marketing techniques. The National Do Not Call Registry and other relevant legislation have reduced true "cold-calling," but cold-calling has not been eliminated as the law has rarely been enforced. Telemarketers have developed a complex system to work around the registry. Of particular note is the fact that charitable organizations are exempt from the regulations on telemarketing. It might surprise some to learn that there is a good deal of money to be made in commissions on nonprofit fund-raising through unsolicited sales techniques.

Daniel worked as a street fund-raiser in Chicago for several children's charities for four to five months. The most well-known was Save the Children. His work at a deli receiving tips via a tip jar is discussed in the companion volume. The following narrative details Daniel's experience receiving commission for street fund-raising.

I would walk up to people in the street and ask them to sponsor a child for $18 a month. We tried to get a two-year commitment from the person.

It was not a bad job. It was stressful at times as you had to keep a level of performance to meet your quota.

I liked the organization. I actually sponsor two kids myself. The money that is raised actually goes to the work of the organization and not to overhead and administration.

I was paid $8 an hour base pay. For one sign-up in a day I received no bonus. For two sign-ups, I received $10 extra; three sign-ups, another $10; four sign-ups, another $20; five sign-ups, another $60. It kept going up. On my best day, I got fourteen sign-ups, and my bonus was $1,400. However, some days I only got one or two. My average was four per day.

It was a good opportunity with low commitment. I felt good about myself, and I could travel. I made good friends with the other people. There was a huge turnover. If you recruited someone who stayed two weeks, you would get a $200 bonus.

They did competitions. If you were the top dialoguer, you would go to another city that had an office. If you had 200 sign-ups, you got a sweatshirt and a bag. If you had 500 sign-ups, you could actually go to a country where they had sponsored kids, such as Ecuador. If you were good, they wanted to keep you.

You need to develop rapport to be good at this job. I approached hundreds of people per day. You got a feel of who was approachable. If they were walking fast and looking down, don't even bother. I had fifteen to twenty people stop and talk on an average day. That is the key. Our strategy was to allow them three excuses which we would try to rebut such as it costs too much money, et cetera. If it went beyond three, you knew it was not going to happen.

We had a lot of training sessions to find out what worked and what did not work.

Nancy worked for Bell South in Memphis, Tennessee, for a summer trying to get new customers and old customers to upgrade their account. This is her story.

I worked with a team of eight people. I was the only person in college. I visited "Mom and Pop"-type businesses ranging from day care centers to small restaurants. I went door-to-door. I tried to get them to extend their contracts or get additional services.

I was paid 100 percent on commission. If a person added voice mail, I would get $5. The biggest commission was for 1,000 minutes per month. For that, I would get $125. The item I sold the most was an extra line. For that, I would get $40. Our quota was to visit 35 businesses per day. Some days I only visited 10 to 15. In a typical day, I would make 2 to 3 sales and earn $50. If I got someone to create a whole new account with most of the bells and whistles such as voice mail, I would get $200. On my best day, I earned $400 in commissions.

I did not like the work. The business was dishonest. It was cheaper for a business to buy unlimited long distance, but we would try to sell them the 1,000-minute package instead because the commission was higher. There were also salespeople who would tell the customer that the service was free when it was not. A lot of salespeople were trying to get promoted into better positions, and that depended upon their sales volume.

In addition, I had to spend a lot of money on gas. The sales area was large, and sometimes I had to travel one and a half hours to get to the location. Furthermore, people took out their frustration with Bell South on you. A lot of people were not nice. My mom did not like what I did because a lady should not be working around in unsafe areas. I did work with a buddy sometimes, and we would split the commission. I used a buddy about one day per week and a lot at the end because I became fearful after being chased by a dog.

However, I learned a lot. In the workshops I learned communication skills and perseverance. I learned not to give up. I got along with all my coworkers. Most were adults who had to support their families. We often went out to dinner after work and laughed about the day's events.

Zenobia canvassed door-to-door for three months for the Democratic National Committee (DNC) during the 2004 election. This is what she had to say about commissions for direct marketing.

I mostly went door-to-door. I also worked the line at Michael Moore's movie, *Fahrenheit 9/11*. I was paid $50 per day for working from 2:30 to 9:00 pm. There was a quota. I got 10 percent for any amount over the quota. The quota depended upon amount raised the night before and the area we were canvassing. The quota was usually between $150 and $200. I went above the quota four out of five days.

I worked the areas of Chevy Chase, MD; Alexandria, VA; Southeast DC; and a few days in Baltimore. When I worked Southeast, the quota was $75. When we worked Bethesda my quota was $200.

We traveled in groups; although we went to each house individually. I gave my basic spiel, and the houses were chosen at random. They could be

Democratic, Republican, or Independent. We did not give out literature as we did not want to be told to come back.

Out of fifty contacts made in a day, I would get money from six of them—12 percent. Usually, I would get $20 per successful contact. The money was given equally in cash or checks. Occasionally, someone would give me a credit card. The larger amounts were paid by check.

We wore T-shirts that had a red DNC on it. Later we were given a badge printed at the office that did not look professional. They were really disorganized.

It is surprising how many people gave money. Sometimes we got money from people we least expected. You can't judge a book by its cover. One Hispanic lady gave me what she said was her last $20. I said don't do that. She said it would come back to her. Another woman in Southeast took $5 out of her bra. My biggest check was for $250, and my biggest cash amount was $50. I usually got 5s and 10s. I had one day where I raised $650. The quota was $150 that day so I made an extra $50.

One person came to the door naked. I told him I would come back later.

One lady in Virginia said, "You know there are a lot of Marine Corp flags around here, and you need to be careful as they are not use to black people." I said, "OK, I won't bother you then." She said, "I'm a Democrat and have been battling with them on Iraq all year."

Jared raises money for U.S. PIRG (Public Interest Research Group) in Washington, D.C. He shared the following story regarding commissions.

I go door-to-door and try to get people to join our organization and to make a financial contribution. PIRG does lobbying and education around environmental issues, helping consumers, and "standing up to powerful interests." This is a summer job. The hours are too long (11 am to 11 pm), and there are some aspects of the organization that are cultlike. You are not going to use my name, right! Everyone is supposed to be happy. The people who work there are OK, but it is too structured for me. I do like the work that they do.

I get a base salary of $300 per week. I am supposed to make $90 a day in contributions or $450 a week. Most know within three days if they are cut out for this. Most leave in this period of time.

We get 34 percent of contributions that are over $450 per week. However, for any one individual contributor, amounts over $150 do not count. The system is a little complex on what counts and what does not count. I essentially earn an extra $100 a week from the commission system.

The organization is pretty fair. People above us do not make above $29,000 per year. About 50 to 60 percent of our contributions go toward overhead such as my salary and the cost of cars to get us out to neighborhoods. It is a great organization for what it does.

In a typical day, I will go to eighty houses, and on average, about four people will donate. The average donation is $25. People are more likely to contribute if they are younger.

I am a field manager and oversee seven others. Because of that, I get $350 per week as my base salary (instead of $300), and I can get 10 percent added onto my commission if the team makes its quota. I have been with the organization for four weeks, and I have made field manager. I will be a junior in college in the fall.

Henry worked for a telemarketing firm in New Jersey for four months. This firm raised money for organizations that claimed to raise money for nonprofit police department athletic and training funds. This is Henry's story in his own words.

It was a scam. One of the police organizations we were supposed to raise money for was in Connecticut. When I visited Connecticut, I called to see if I could visit the training facility. It ended up being someone's house. When I got back to the firm, they told me to never do that again.

The job was funny in that I got a lot of good stories, but the job itself was not fun.

I was paid $7.50 an hour. In a four-hour shift, I made 400 calls of which I would talk to about 200 people. Success depended a lot upon the day and the state. When I called Boston, I put on a fake Boston accent and did well. On average, five to ten people a day said they would make a donation. The average donation was $10. We did not take credit cards on the telephone. We would send them a pledge envelope and a police sticker, and about 85 percent of the pledges came back with money.

If 50 percent of my pledges for a month came back with money, I would get a 50¢ raise to $8.00. This could continue going up. Some people at the firm made $14 an hour.

They were always hiring. There was very big turnover.

Cathy worked for a telemarketing firm during the summer while she was on vacation from college. This is her story.

I was in Florida, and we sold subscriptions to the *New York Times*. I did not like working for this firm. I simply did not like selling things. When I resigned at the end of the summer, I sent a nasty letter about emotional and mental anguish and how I could not continue.

I received a base rate of $7.25 an hour. If we sold three subscriptions in an hour, our base rate for that hour increased to $10.75. I never sold three subscriptions in an hour.

We also had team competitions. There were ten to thirteen of us in a team, and there were five teams. If we sold the most in our team, we would get a bonus. There were different competitions within the team. If our team sold the most in a month, our entire team would get a $1 an hour increase for that month.

After the first week, I was burned out. The firm made most of their money by training people. They were happy to fire you after the training because they were paid for training. There was massive turnover. If I recruited someone who stayed thirty days, I would get a $300 bonus. I never did that either.

Theresa worked as a telemarketer for a Shakespeare Theatre for three months. Her job as a server in a restaurant is discussed elsewhere. The following narrative illustrates Theresa's perspective on commissions for direct marketing.

The job was OK until the bosses started to bring in their dogs. I am scared of some types of dogs. They fired me because I complained. The job was also very tedious.

I was paid $7.50 an hour. I called customers who had bought tickets in the past. We had two types of bonuses. There was a collective bonus of $5 or so if we made our collective goal for the day. I also got $1.50 for people who bought tickets for the banquet or donated over $150 so their names would get into the catalog. I averaged only two big sales a week. I also got two free tickets to see Shakespeare, whom I really love.

I made 100 to 300 calls a day. Thirty to forty percent of people would buy something. Remember, these were people who bought tickets in the past. If I was calling people who had not purchased tickets in several years, my success rate was only around 10 percent.

Nalini has had two jobs for which she was paid commission. She worked as a telemarketer and a bill collector. Nalini shared the following stories regarding her experience with commission systems.

I worked for three months for a telemarketing firm in Houston, Texas, selling medical equipment to hospitals. I hated it. We tried to sell hospitals everyday items such as syringes, bandages, and IVs. You are trying to sell to people who already had established vendors for these items. I would try to talk to the director of the hospital. If I could not talk to the director, I would talk to whoever answered the phone and try to talk to whoever could help me.

I had a computer that would tell me who to call. I made 200 to 300 calls a day. I would talk to ten people on an average day; of which, three said they would consider it and call me back. In three months, I never got an order, so I quit.

I was paid $12.75 an hour. My commission would have been 10 percent, and it would have gone up if I sold more than $10,000 to any one hospital.

I worked as a bill collector for seven months. I hated this job but not as much as the other telemarketing firm. At least I made commission. I was paid $8.50 an hour. The names we called were totally random. One call could be for someone who owed Sears $500. The next could be someone who owed a gas station $20, and the next could be for someone who owed a hospital $25,000.

I made 60 to 100 calls a day, and I would talk to a person about half the time. A lot of people had caller IDs that would automatically block my call. About three to five people per day would make a payment.

I was paid 5 percent commission. If someone owed Sears $500, I would get $25.00 if they sent the payment directly to Sears, sent it to me, gave me a credit card or check over the phone, or made some other payment arrangement. I would set up installment plans for big hospital bills (say $200 a month). As long as they continued paying, I would get my commission.

I was paid bi-weekly. I never knew how much I would get because I did not get my commission until the person paid. Usually there would be an extra $200 to $300 per paycheck from my commission. It was a nice surprise. If I made a lot on commission, they would have me working bigger accounts (over $50,000). I never got moved up.

The job was easy, but there was a lot of turnover because many people did not get a lot of commission.

Raisha sold knives for six months to add to her college fund. This is her story.

I was a traveling salesperson in California. I sort of liked the job. The money was OK, but we had a lot of retreats, required regional meetings, group activities, chanting, and people smiling. I did not like any of that.

I had a base salary of $17.25 per hour that kicked in if the commission was too low. This hourly wage was only for when I actually had a sales visit. Most sales visits lasted about an hour. The rate might seem high, but the cost of living was high in California, and it did not cover travel time. The person you were visiting had to sign a form saying that the sales visit had occurred.

After the first month, I was strictly on commission. I received 10 to 15 percent of the total sales price. The typical sale was a three piece knife set for $250 to $300. I make a sale 49 percent of the time. It took about an hour to make this sale. I got paid every two weeks. The commissions were a little complicated, and I still get $10 a month or so from sales that were a year ago. I don't quite understand how the system worked.

Most of my sales started with family and friends. Then I asked them for referrals and asked the referrals for referrals. I never gave any money back to the referrals. That seems a little cold, doesn't it?

Some people made a lot of money selling knives. I liked making my own choice. If I worked hard, I could do OK. However, I don't like working mostly for commissions.

Dorothy sold insurance door-to-door for a year in Maine. Her other jobs selling Volvos and Sear's appliances are included elsewhere in this volume. The following narrative details Dorothy's experience receiving commission for direct marketing.

I sold supplemental and life insurance. This was based upon residual income. You got a percentage as long as the person kept the policy. If you stayed on for more than a year, you could do very well.

The structure for all the policies was fairly similar. Upon sale of the policy, you would get the first two months payments. After that, you would get 10 percent every month. An accident policy would cost $20 per month, life insurance $200 per month, and a whole family account could be $400 per month.

The selling was literally door-to-door. On a typical day, I would knock on forty doors. Guys would get in the door perhaps twice. I was a girl and was less threatening, so I would get in about ten of those doors. I would sell thirty policies a month on a good month. If I was on a roll, I could average $2,000 to $3,000 a week without taking into account the residual. If I stayed with the company, I would have done very well.

I left because dealing with claims was very rough. I would hear about how people died, and I might have to tell them they were not covered. There were a lot of loopholes. It was awful. I was sometimes fighting the company. I did not want to be the bad guy.

Samuel had two types of jobs working on commission. He worked as a telemarketer petitioning potential customers to schedule appointments for an ADT Security sales agent to make a face-to-face pitch, and he currently sells ads on the Internet. His job as a server is included in the companion volume on tipping norms. The following illustrates Samuel's experiences receiving commissions for his work in direct marketing.

I worked as a telemarketer for one and a half years while I was in high school. I was paid $8 an hour to try to set up appointments for salesmen to go to people's houses for ADT Security. The job was very boring and annoying but paid well for a high school student.

It was very difficult to make the commission. I made 400 calls a day. If I got four legitimate leads, I would get $20. If I got eight leads, I would get $40 to $50. A legitimate lead was when the salesman called back and made an appointment with an eligible household. I got commission less than 10 percent of the time. We were really working just to keep our jobs and not for commission. We were expected to get two real leads per day.

We were all in high school or college and got along pretty well. The manager tried to set up competition—"Joe got six leads today. How come you only got two?"

I now sell ads on the Internet. I have my own Web site, which is mostly hip-hop. There are four ways to make money.

CPM is cost per meal [Note: On the Internet, this is called cost through model or cost per thousand], and you get 8¢ to $1 for every time an ad appears on their screen. This is for new movies or for brand recognition like Nike. The person does not have to do anything active. The ad merely appears.

CPC is cost per click. I can get between 20¢ and $4. The person actually clicks on the ad. A lot of these are for entertainment sites and are very common.

CPL is cost per load. The person puts their e-mail or address into a form. This is mostly for stores. They could be selling computers, eBay, or whatever. You can get 50¢ plus for these.

CPA is cost per action. The person makes a purchase—here you get a commission. For adult entertainment sites the commission is very high. If it is a monthly sub—say $20 a month—you get half for as long as the person continues their subscription. Bigger companies will have much smaller commissions. Amazon's is about 7 percent.

From all of these, I make $1,500 a month with a part-time job. I am more of a marketer than a programmer. I pay $350 a month to maintain my site. I am trying to branch out and develop a joke Web site or nonentertainment sites. It is very competitive in the entertainment sites. It would be good to get into lawyer sites. At one point, lawyers were paying $1,000 for cost per clicks for people who were looking for a type of cancer—mesothelioma!

About half of my revenue comes from third-party sites such as Yahoo or Google. They send me a check each month. Others pay me directly via Pay-Pal. I also make $50 a month from some whose ads are on my site.

Eighty percent of my hits come from people searching on Google or other search engines. As more people hit my Web site, my rating goes up, and for some searches, I come up on the first page. This is what you want—to keep building and building.

I am about to start selling CDs that are given to disc jockeys by music companies as special compilations used for promotions. I will buy them from the DJs for $2 or $3 and sell them for $5 or $6.

Bonnie has worked in several capacities at Arbitron. She was also interviewed about her job as a book buyer.

Arbitron determines market share for radio stations. Market share helps determine advertising rates. Recently, they began using Portable People Meters (PPM), which are devices that people wear and can determine what they are listening to.

People in the call center earn a good wage—$16.50 an hour plus full benefits. Most work part-time (twenty-two hours a week). The work is hard because there are a lot of rules. It is not fun.

The bonus system is fairly complex. Essentially, you are paid by some combination of success rate, number of calls, and type of calls. The initial call is sample preparation, and the caller attempts to get people to agree to receive the literature. Later calls are to get them to agree to participate. Other calls are to help them use the equipment and to stay in the program. The biggest bonus is based upon people agreeing to install the meter.

Managers have a big affect on your commission structure. If they give you a list of those whose numbers have been busy or no answer, you are unlikely to get many successful calls. On the other hand, people who said to call back are likely to agree to participate. Some callers are allowed to cherry-pick.

A couple of years ago they drastically increased the amount of money you could receive from bonuses. The result was a disaster, and morale went way down. People began cheating. They would say someone agreed when they did not. If your success rate was below 50 percent, you received no bonus. Therefore, some people would say the person agreed to get called back instead of saying it was a refusal.

Furthermore, other departments were affected. You might say a senile old man agreed to participate. The installation department would spend a lot of time and money setting up the equipment, only to realize it was for naught. Department goals can definitely conflict.

Arbitron recently scaled back parts of the bonus system, and people who use to game the system are pissed. It is very hard to find a good system to incentivize employees.

The typical part-time worker (twenty-two hours a week) will earn $1,400 a month in direct pay. Some were earning $2,000 in bonuses by gaming the system. The average bonus was probably $200. However, one of our best employees got nothing as her refusal rate was greater than 50 percent. She refused to be dishonest.

There are a number of themes evident in the narratives regarding commissions for direct marketing techniques. Door-to-door sales have some unique challenges for men and women. Men are more likely to be perceived as a potential threat, which might negatively impact their sales or implore them to work in mixed-gender teams that might result in a split commission. Alternatively, women are more likely to feel threatened or at risk, which might negatively impact their sales or require them to incur additional costs to increase their safety. In any case, there are a number of risk factors and additional costs associated with door-to-door sales.

Several of the responses indicate that the more control workers feel over their ability to affect their work (e.g., flexible schedules, pay that reflects work effort, products they feel good about selling, etc.), the less likely they are to be dissatisfied with their job. Furthermore, turnover is likely higher when the commissions are perceived to be unattainable. It is also interesting to note that the respondents were much more likely to be unhappy with the job when the product was less than credible or lacking merit in their mind. When product confidence is low, selling is more difficult, and a sense of accomplishment may also be lacking for some.

One pattern that appears to crop up periodically across job categories is that even when people do not clearly understand how the system works, they do not seem to express much mistrust in the calculation of their compensation. Although, it is difficult to distinguish a trust in the commission system versus resignation or acquiescence. Direct marketing has another thing in common with commission systems in several of the other job categories. The commission structure pushes out those who are not well-suited for sales. In fact, Bonnie's experience at Arbitron illustrates not only this point but the intersection of structure and craft in management. The commission structure at Arbitron is intended to reward those with the lowest refusal rate by affording them a commission and call lists that offer greater sales potential. But based on Bonnie's description, there were at least two problems that interfered with the adequate translation of these incentives. First, because the commission structure was complex and the bonus excessive, employees perceived the reward to be out of reach. Some employees cheated, and the commission structure ended up rewarding them. And, honest employees lost faith in the system. Second, when people figured out how to game the system, managers were not using their discretion to reward the employees who had the potential to establish credibility in the product. When managers depend upon the productivity of their workforce to elicit their own commissions and bonuses, they have an incentive to reward results regardless of the credibility of the sales. Incentive schemes that hold managers accountable for productivity over the long term and reward sales staff for consistently credible results are more sustainable than those that simply inflate statistics to give the appearance of profitability.

6

Clothes, Jewelry, and Cosmetics

How honest is the sales associate when she or he tells you that those shoes are perfect for you? To what extent is she or he interested in "customer service" (i.e., helping to make the best choice for you)? If she or he makes very few sales, she or he is unlikely to keep her or his job, but does she or he have a more immediate reason for completing the sale? Is she or he getting a commission? How do retail sales commissions affect the behavior of the sales associates?

There were 1,836,000 retail salespeople in the United States who earned an average of $32,000 in 2008 according to the Census Bureau. The Bureau of Labor Statistics regularly reports high expectations regarding employment opportunities in this sector due to a consistent need to replace the large number of workers who leave the occupation each year. Clothes, jewelry, and cosmetics retailers typically want to promote courteous, efficient service and attempt to structure compensation for their sales force to maximize this type of service. Compensation systems vary considerably by the business, specific type and quality of the merchandise sold, and the location. People who sell clothes, jewelry, and cosmetics may make an hourly wage, a commission, or some combination of both. When salespeople make a commission, they get a percentage of the sales attributed to them.

Raquel is the district manager for a clothing chain that caters to larger women. She shared the following story regarding the commission system.

I've been at this store for six years and have been in clothing all my life. I like it—after all, it is all that I know at this point. I recruit and hire managers, and I'm in charge of inventory. You cannot use the name of the store.

I get salary and bonus. My salary is about $80,000 per year. My bonus is computed each month. If sales are 6 percent higher than last year for a particular month, I get $70 for each of the fifteen or so stores that I oversee. This progresses up to 40 percent; in which case, I would get $600. All fifteen stores are evaluated each month. Last year, I made around $8,000 in bonuses. The bonuses can be reduced if there are losses (theft) of over 3 percent at a store.

Each store manager has the same incentive program that I do. The difference is that for a store manager the program only applies to their store, and the amounts are doubled. Therefore, if sales are 6 percent higher over last year for any one month, they would get $140. The assistant managers are also on the same bonus system, but their amounts are not doubled.

Sales associates are paid by the hour and have no commission. They can get $3 for every store credit card that is opened, and there are some other incentives throughout the course of the year.

For me, the bonus is a better incentive than my yearly increase in salary. Because I get the bonus each month, there is immediate gratification. In addition, you can have a bad year but still have a couple of good months. That really helps.

Fran works for a medical supply company in Florida and shared the following story.

I work for the division that sells to women who are survivors of breast cancer. I do not like my job. I don't have the aggression necessary to be a good salesperson. I am a single parent, and I need the job. I have been miserable for the five years that I have worked in this position.

I get paid $11 an hour. The commission structure is really complicated. I have to sell over $25,000 in products per month to get a commission. It maxes out at 4 percent when sales are above $40,000. It is a lower percent at $25,000. In an average month, I make $1,200 in commission. During my best month, I made $2,500 in commission.

There are bonuses for managers but not for me.

We put ads in papers, and women call to request a catalog. I call these women. I make 100 to 150 calls a day and talk to forty women daily. I probably average twelve sales a day. The average sale is for six bras and a prosthetic (a form in the bra). This averages out to $350.

The competition among the sales staff can be cutthroat. Once you speak to a customer, that customer is supposed to be yours. However, if you are not there when she calls back, people will try to steal the order. It can get ugly sometimes. I don't exchange bad words because I want to keep my job. Our department is all women, and that is not a good thing. On a 1–10 scale, we are a 6. We are civil.

The work can be very depressing. A lot of the women are over sixty-five and have many ailments. I spoke to a woman a few days ago who couldn't talk because she was on her way out to her husband's funeral. It is a depressing position.

Lee has been working at a Nordstrom's in the Washington, D.C., area for the last six months. This is what Lee had to say about commissions in clothing sales.

I work in the Brass Plum department. We sell clothes to junior teens. I don't like the commission structure.

My base salary is $9 an hour. I am supposed to sell $225 worth of clothes per hour. If I work an eight-hour day, I am supposed to sell $1,800 worth. Any amount over that, I get 9 percent commission. I work Friday, Saturday, and Sunday. Saturday is usually a good day. Friday and Sunday are slow. If I don't make my draw on all three days, I don't get a commission. I did not receive a commission on any week over the last month.

Christmas was good. On my best week, I got 6 percent of $2,700 ($162). They reduced the draw rate during this time period.

It is very competitive with the other sales staff. You might run out to get clothes for a customer, and another person will try to ring up the sale while you are gone. I politely tell them that it is my customer. I have not had to go to the manager. Among other coworkers, it has gotten pretty ugly.

The amount we are expected to sell is ridiculous because other than Christmas, sales are slow.

Betsy worked for a year selling clothes at Ralph Lauren in Washington, D.C. The following narrative details her perspective on the commission system in clothing sales.

Ralph Lauren sells high-end clothes. You can get a jacket for $3,000. I did not enjoy it. It was a commission-based job with a lot of competition. There was a lot of pressure to sell and be the first to greet the person entering the store. It was hard to be friends with your coworkers.

I was paid $6.25 an hour. I was expected to sell $175 per hour. Any amount over that, I would get 20 percent commission. If I did not make my quota, I would make my salary. I was given two weeks to make my goal. If I was below my goal, I could theoretically not even get my base salary. If people returned goods, that counted against me.

In a forty-hour week, I averaged $300. I did better working on the weekends. My best week was around the holidays when I made $600. It is good to be in that business around the holidays.

The competition with the staff was cutthroat. There were often words between employees, verbal fights, and complaints to management. People would try to steal customers who were already greeted. You could not share commissions. A lot of enemies were made. My worst enemy to date still works at the store. I'm embarrassed to say that we had a verbal fight, and I am a very mellow person.

The best customers were wealthy regulars. There were some customers who came in once a week or once a month and spent $3,000. More senior sales staff would have some of these customers as their base. Younger women were harder sales. We wanted mature women with rich husbands or a lot of their own money. High school kids looking for Polo Shirts were harder.

Women only sold to women, and men sold to men. There could be a lot of confusion ringing up sales if a woman bought something for herself and then a tie for her husband.

Eric worked as a store manager for Brooks Brothers for eight years. His work for a pest management company is presented elsewhere. The following narrative details Eric's experiences receiving commission as a clothing store manager.

I liked working for Brooks Brothers, but the store owned you on weekends. This became a real problem once I had a child. I wanted a life.

A senior salesperson gets $14 an hour plus commissions. The commission structure is complicated. You get 2 ⅛ percent on all sales. This can go up depending upon your sales quota. The sales quota is based upon sales from the year before. If you reach 70 percent of your threshold, you get an extra 0.625 (2.125 percent + 0.0625 = 2.1875 percent). This goes up in different steps up to 5 percent.

In my best year, I had $1 million in business and made $70,000. After that, the dot com bust occurred, and sales went down.

I was a manager for several years. I had a salary of about $70,000. I also got bonuses each quarter depending upon how the store did. We had monthly quotas. These bonuses ranged from $2,500 to $7,000. We had monthly quotas, but I did not do sales when I was a manager.

Brooks Brothers has two types of stores: union and non-union. Union stores have closed floors. With closed floors, there are essentially three departments: ladies, men's tailored, and furnishings. If I am in furnishings and someone comes in asking for a suit, I can't help them. If they ask for me directly or first buy a shirt from me, then I can help them with a suit. There is more competition among the sales staff with open floors. Any salesperson can sell to anyone. When I was a manager, it sometimes seemed that I was babysitting a bunch of kids. They would fight about the commissions. "I saw the person first." "No! I saw him first," and so on. It could get ugly, and there were occasional arguments in front of the customers. This was another reason why I left.

Owen has worked for the past ten months at the Men's Warehouse, a clothing store in the Washington, D.C., area. This is his story.

The job is pretty good. I enjoy working with the public. I also like the challenge of selling things. I get to read my customer.

I earn $5 an hour plus commission. The commission ranges from 3.5 percent to 10 percent. Shirts and socks have 3.5 percent commissions, and suits and shoes have a commission of 10 percent. If I sell over $600 in any one sale, I am guaranteed a commission of at least 6 percent. It can get a little complicated.

I average $250 to $300 a week in commission, and I work a twenty-five-hour week. My best week ever was when I made $730.

There is competition among the sales staff, which can sometimes get ugly. I used to work at another Men's Warehouse, which was more dog-eat-dog. If you left for the bathroom, you could have a sale stolen. The manager of the present store rotates us as customers come in the door. Even if a customer stays a long time, I would get the next customer. It is much more fair, having a system.

When I first started, I was not paid commission. I was slipped money under the table when the sale was credited to someone else. If a salesperson made $8, he would slip me $2. This was not a formal policy.

I sell a lot. However, my boss gave me the hint that what mattered was not how much you sold, but what you sold. We guide customers to the items that give us a higher commission. We make higher commission on sales items. Therefore, we sometimes steer people away from the high-priced suits to the sales rack.

When people return items, they take money from our base pay for the next pay period, not our commission sales. Therefore, it does not hurt as much.

Tanisha has worked for the last five months at Ann Taylor, a clothing store for women. This is her story.

I like working there. I like the staff and the working environment. It is very laid back.

I am paid $9 per hour. I am supposed to sell $400 of clothing per hour. For any amount that I sell over the quota, I get 2 percent. This is calculated on a monthly basis. If I work 80 hours per month, I get 2 percent of any sales over $32,000. I've never made this amount. Some of the full-time people make it. They have more experience or are more focused.

The managers encourage competition among the staff. There are no real hard feelings if someone is aggressive.

I'm not really interested in making the commission sales. I'm focused on my hourly wages so that I can be a student.

Billie works at the shoe department at a Nordstrom's in the Washington, D.C., area. He shared the following story regarding commissions.

I love working on commission. It is better than hourly. I work well with people, and I am good at persuasion.

I work strictly on commission, and I get 10 percent of sales. I used to work in a department at Nordstrom's that sold to young men (thirty-year-olds), and the commission was 5.75 percent. I also worked in a clothing department for women at Nordstrom's. My status was seasonal at the time, and I got a commission of 5.75 percent. People who were full-time received 6.75 percent. If they met their goal, their percentage would go up.

The three departments gave me about the same paycheck. I get about $20 per hour. I work really hard. If I have a bad week, I get $13 per hour, which is the goal set by Nordstrom's. If you did not meet your goal, you could fall back on the theoretical base pay of $7 or $8. Nordstrom's is attempting to get rid of the base pay.

It is harder to sell shoes than clothes. Men are easier than women. They are not indecisive. They know what they want, and they just buy it. The women's clothing is more expensive, and that is why the percentage is the same as the men's.

If there are returns, they are taken out of our current commission. For example, if I sell $20,000 worth of clothing in a month and have $5,000 in returns, I get commission on $15,000.

There is competition among the sales staff. If you steal customers, you can make more money. However, it is uncomfortable. I want to get along. It works better for you if you don't steal. It is less hassle. If someone does steal, they get the sale. They might be respected for it because they are there to get money. There are no fights. Usually nothing is said. Once I worked with someone else's customer by mistake. When I was told that I had taken someone else's customer, I apologized. We cannot share commissions.

Commissions are not for everyone. If you are shy or reserved, you won't like it. I like knowing that if I work hard, I earn more by applying my personality. The sky is my limit. I don't like working for a base pay. Having just a base pay is not a great option for me.

Mark was the assistant manager of a shoe store in Allentown, Pennsylvania. This is his story in his own words.

I've worked there for five years. I am going to school now. We sold all types of shoes. It wasn't really high end. The most expensive shoes were Timberlands for $110. When I go back home for vacation, I work for the store. I liked working at the store. It was boring and mundane, but I liked my coworkers.

I got paid $9.50 an hour plus 2 percent of my sales. Because of the commission, I usually got $11.00 to $11.50 an hour instead of $9.50. I usually sold $900 worth of shoes a day. It really ranged. Because I was assistant manager, I got a higher hourly wage than the other salespeople. The regular salespeople got 7 percent commissions or minimum wage ($5.15 an hour), whichever was higher. They almost always got more than the minimum wage.

Commission sales were really an easy way to make more money. It was easy to bump my salary up.

There was enough business to go around, so we did not really compete. It was not a real problem.

I would rather wait on men than women. They were easier. Women's styles were hard at times. "Do you like the navy with the silver trim?" "I don't wear silver, so I don't know."

Linda has worked as a salesperson at a boutique in the Soho district of New York City. This is what she had to say about commissions.

The store sells jewelry, bags, and some clothing. I have worked in the store for the past two months. I like my job, but I am about to quit to take a job with higher pay that is more in line with my schooling.

I am paid $12 an hour and receive a 3 percent commission on sales. The computer attached to the cash register records my sales, and I am paid every two weeks. In a typical nine-hour shift before Christmas, I made about $80 on a good day from commissions. Now that the holidays are past, I average $20 to $30 a day.

When a person returns an item, they can only get in-store credit. Therefore, this does not affect my commissions.

Commissions make the job more competitive. There are five other sales-people. The person who rings the sales up gets the commission. Sometimes it is simply a matter of who is closest to the register. This sometimes creates a lot of tension, but the job is more exciting than my previous sales job at Abercrombie and Fitch where there were no commissions. At Abercrombie, the salespeople were more laid back, and there was less of an attempt to talk customers into buying things. Even so, I like working at the boutique better.

At the boutique store, there is one girl who tries to take sales away from other salespeople. She is not well-liked.

Brian has sold fine jewelry in Bloomingdale's for the past six years. He shared the following story.

I like my coworkers, and I have also become good friends with some of my customers. But, this is not what I set out to do when I finished college. In addition, jewelry is not my thing. It is not my cup of tea, but I like it when I'm selling.

I get $11.50 an hour. You are not going to use my name, right? I get a 2 percent commission on all sales. In a typical week, I sell $5,000 to $6,000 of jewelry. Around Christmas, this goes up to $25,000. Valentine's Day and Mother's Day are also good sales weeks. My best month was around Christmas when I sold $100,000 of jewelry. That was nice.

You have to fight for your sales. If there are three of us working, you have to try not to push someone out of the way. We try to let other salespeople finish sales once they start. We occasionally ring up for another salesperson when a person comes back. However, if you put a fair amount of your own time into the sale, you will keep the sale. There is no sharing of commissions. Our department is OK. We used to have someone who tried to take all the sales for himself. There was a lot of friction, and it was not resolved. We took more of his sales in retaliation. It was not a good work environment. He is no longer here.

When someone exchanges an item, the return counts against your next paycheck. However, if the person uses the credit, the person who makes the next transaction gets the commission. It can be demoralizing when someone makes returns when you really worked with him. There are some people who will buy something to wear at a special event and then they return it the next week. You know when someone buys a $5,000 item in five minutes that it is likely coming back. It is rough because they can return it at any store. One day, I sold $4,500 in one day and later found out that at another store some-one returned $7,000 of my sales. This happened on the same day. About 25 percent of my sales get returned.

Some days you have zero sales. However, one customer can make your day.

John worked for a year and a half for Zale's jewelers. This is his story.

I liked working there. It was my first retail job. It was good around holidays, but you really had to rely upon your base pay at other times.

My base pay was $7.50 an hour. I also made 1 percent commission on all sales. If I met my yearly quota ($300,000), I would get 2 percent commission. This 2 percent would also cover the sales between $0 and $300,000. If we did not meet our quota, we got a big lecture and would probably have to attend a sales class. People who worked part-time had a lower quota. If you were semi–part-time (thirty hours), it was really difficult to make the quota.

I was over quota. I was good at what I did. I averaged $600 every two weeks for my commission. My highest commission check was $900. You could do well around Valentine's Day, Mother's Day, and Christmas.

There was competition among the sales staff. More experienced workers would work the system. Two females who had been there for over five years would deliberately linger around the diamond counter when they should have been near the door. It made it very difficult. You have to voice your opinion or get walked all over. The store was female-dominated. I was the only male. It was hard to bring up the issue. I talked to the manager but was mostly ignored.

There was no real sharing of commissions. However, if you started a sale one day and the person came back another day and closed it with someone else, you could split the commission.

You did not have to give the commission back with returns. However, returned sales would not count toward your quota. About 5 to 10 percent of the customers would return the items.

I now work at Bed, Bath, and Beyond. We don't have commissions. I like that better. I don't have to have the urge to make quota. I come in and do my duties.

Ann is a makeup artist in California and sells cosmetics. She shared the following story about commissions.

I work for the product line Benefit. I've been doing it for a year, and I like it. I've wanted to work with makeup for several years. The counter I work for is in a Macy's store. Both Benefit and Macy's pay me in one paycheck. I don't know how they split it up.

I can't tell you how much I make, but it is approximately $9.50 an hour. I also get 3 percent commission on all sales. An average day is about $500 in sales. A really good day is about $1,000, and a bad day is around $300.

We don't share our commissions.

Our product line is not that competitive. We help each other. At other product lines it can be much more cutthroat. This usually happens with a senior person when a younger person joins the counter.

We are not allowed to take tips. However, when I do makeovers, I sometimes get offered a tip. I see about fifty or so customers a week. Maybe two people a month will offer me $5 or $10.

All the lines at Macy's are on commission except Mac. Mac is straight salary.

Patti has had three different jobs working commissions. She sold hair removal and skin rejuvenation procedures. She sold cosmetics at a department store, and she sold Mary Kay products. The following narrative illustrates Patti's perspective on commission systems.

I have been the manager for the past six months for a clinic that performs hair removal and skin rejuvenation. I work a lot of hours—about sixty hours per week both managing the clinic and going to shows on the weekend. I have kids ranging from age eight to sixteen, and I often bring them with me to the shows.

I have a salary of $45,000 per year. I also make commission. If I sell over $55,000 of procedures per month, I get 2 percent of the $55,000. This is a sliding scale. For example, at $60,000 to $65,000 a month I get 2.5 percent. I know of one person at another clinic who sold $176,000 in a month and got 9 percent. I also try to get people to upscale their service. If they are coming in for a bikini waxing, I will suggest underarm waxing.

I have made the minimum for four months. I go to events, set up a table, pass out literature, and talk to people. At a recent travel expo, I got 115 leads and a lot more from a bridal show. We often have a box for a drawing. The first prize is a $1,500 package. Given the leads, a call center calls to set up appointments for consultations.

I don't share commissions with anyone. However, the nurse practitioner can also get a commission if they get someone to upscale as long as the clinic makes its $55,000 limit.

Upper lifts cost $600 for six sessions and a two-year guarantee. Our most expensive item is a full-body for $13,000. Bikini lines cost $440. Our most popular item for women is bikini underarms for women at $2,800 and men's backs for $2,700. There are five of us who work at the clinic.

Today, we have nonstop appointments for procedures from 8:00 am to 8:00 pm. Most of these are people coming back for additional treatments. I also have three or four consults today.

Last month, the call center booked 151 appointments. Eighty showed, 37 did not show, and 34 cancelled. Of the 80 who showed, 36 purchased treatments worth $56,000. The month before, I did not make the $55,000 threshold.

On really slow days, I will go to grocery stores and pass out cards. I like being a salesperson.

I also worked for six months at a cosmetic counter at Lord & Taylor's. I quit when I got recruited for my job at the clinic. I worked thirty-four hours per week. I started at $7.25 an hour and left at $10.50 an hour.

I got 3 percent of all sales. There was no threshold. I got promoted to counter manager, and also made 1 percent of all sales for that counter (an Estée Lauder product) when sold by another salesperson. If I sold another line, I would get 2 percent. I averaged $100 every two weeks in commissions. I did not share these commissions.

When times were slow, I did events. I did makeovers, gave people foundations, and went to schools around prom time.

I loved working the counter. I'm a people person.

There was a lot of competition among the staff. It most definitely could get vicious at times. When times were slow, we would all compete. I would go to the stock room, and someone would try to sell to my client.

Lord & Taylor's compares you to that day during the previous year. If the person who had your position a year ago sold $300 on that day, then you should sell $325.

On average, about half of the people I show a product will buy. It really helps if I can give free samples. If I can make a woman feel good about herself, she will buy. If she feels good, I will tell her to also look at another product. "See what it can do for you?" Sales work is a lot of fun but also a lot of pressure.

[Patti sold Mary Kay cosmetics for three years as well.] This was 100 percent commission. I had to be much more aggressive. I would try to find people in stores and give them my card. If they were interested, I called them back and suggested that they try to invite over a few of their girlfriends for a pampering session.

My commission was 50 percent. In a typical month, I earned between $300 and $1,000 per month. I had to pay for my merchandise in advance, and I would pay for all my samples. Samples cost $25 to $50 per month. I made the most around holidays. During my most lucrative month I made $3,000. I could sell $500 in one day with gift packages. It took me three hours to put the packages together. I did three to four groups per month, and the typical group had five to six people. About half my sales were through groups, and the other half to individuals.

I sold a lot around Mother's Day and Valentine's Day. I went to the ship-yard in Virginia and opened the back of my truck. Men don't like to shop, and I could do very well.

It was a lot of fun. I met a lot of people. I liked the way women felt after they were all made up. Women buy on emotion. If they feel good, they buy.

Michelle sells romantic products for women via a company called Slumber Parties. She also makes bonuses for her work at an Old Navy clothing store. These are her experiences with commission systems.

I've been doing this for five months, and I love it. I am a manager at an Old Navy store, and I am about to quit that and sell romantic products full time. It is a lot of fun and is certainly the most fun I have ever had in a job.

We have the equivalent of Tupperware parties. I sell lotions, creams, and sex toys. We are about empowering women's sexuality. Our biggest sales products are vibrators, but it depends upon the group. A typical sales session will last two to five hours.

I purchase the products at a discounted rate (30 to 50 percent off) and sell them at retail. They are all Slumber Party products. I get all my business via word-of-mouth, and at each party, I try to get two attendees to host an additional party. The parties average ten guests with as many as twenty-five. Ninety percent of people at a party will buy something, and the average sale is $75.

The hostess gets 10 percent of my total sales toward the purchase of her own products. So if I sell $1,000, she can get $100 worth of free products. She is responsible for getting people to the parties.

I never get any tips. It is also impossible to predict who will buy the most.

I would like to do three or four parties per week, but I can't because of the time pressures of my other job.

I have had very little grief from people so far. It has been fun. The work depends upon you. The company has great support, but it is up to you to put in as much as you want to get out.

I am now a store manager at Old Navy. I used to really like this job, but the time pressures are too much for having a normal family life. I work ten to twelve hours a day. I am paid straight salary. Managers at Old Navy earn between $40,000 and $50,000 a year. No one at Old Navy gets commissions. However, I get bonuses.

The bonus is up to $400 a month and is dependent upon reaching certain goals. These sales goals are based on increases in sales compared to last year's sales for the same month. It is hard to achieve the goal. On average, I get the bonus four to five months per year.

Kal has been buying gold jewelry for the past two years. He is not selling a product, so it is difficult to determine where exactly his experience is best categorized. Is his experience with commissions akin to the financial sector, jewelry, or miscellaneous? Kal's story is included below.

I love what I do. I interact with people on a daily basis. I help people. They get the cash they need in a bad economy.

In a typical transaction, I go to a person's house and bring my scale and various acids. The acids allow me to determine the purity of the gold. I sort the jewelry by carets, weigh it, and buy by the penny-weight (20 penny-weights = 1 troy ounce). I pay the person cash. I will buy a typical male wedding ban for $50. The average person will sell me between $500 and $800 in jewelry. My biggest sale was for $23,000. Of over 2,000 people I have seen, less than 20 did not sell me their gold. Most thought they would get less than what I actually gave them.

I sell the gold to a refiner who melts it down. My markup is between 20 percent and 40 percent. In most cases, it is closer to 40 percent, and in some situations, it will be higher. The markup is higher when buying is inconvenient because the amount sold is low or the location is very difficult to get at. My markup is not as high as other people in the business as I go direct to a refiner, and it does not have to go through a third person.

If you purchase a piece of gold jewelry for $500, I will purchase it from you for $75 and sell it to a refiner for $100.

In a typical gold party, five friends come over, and food and wine is served. The host gets 10 percent of my gross. When I started out, 70 percent of my sales were from parties, but as you finish going through your friends, it is hard to find other people to host parties. Now, 80 percent of my sales are directly from individuals. All my sales are from word-of-mouth. I give 10 percent of my gross to people who refer me to other people.

My ideal client is a woman between the ages of fifty and eighty. Younger women have less gold, and poor women have gold of lower quality.

I will also melt down silver and platinum. If a person has a stone in the jewelry, I will remove it. I will also broker the stones and other jewelry such as watches. I will take the jewelry to "my guy," and if he offers me $5,000, I will offer the client $4,500.

I am licensed, and I must hold the gold for fifteen days before bringing it to a refiner. I have to fill out a variety of forms for each transaction. If I am concerned that the price of gold will drop in those fifteen days, I can sell it on the future's market. The great thing about gold is that it will never degrade. Ninety-five percent of gold ever mined still exists.

The biggest problem with buying gold is security. You bring a lot of cash with your to purchase gold. You need to keep safe.

The variation in commission structures in clothes, jewelry, and cosmetics sales is tremendous. There is not only a considerable degree of variation and complexity, but the tracking of commissions is labor-intensive (although often computerized). One of the noteworthy aspects of tracking commissions that this chapter brings to light is the fact that a sales associate is unlikely to be able to keep track of his or her own commissions; yet the systems tend to retain a reasonable degree of credibility. Future research may explore the extent to which this trust is extended to the company, computers, and/or others in general.

It is fascinating that sales associates draw conclusions about customer characteristics without accounting for differences in price or circumstance. For example, Billie stated fairly conclusively that women are more "indecisive," and while he noted that items sold to women at Nordstrom's tend to be more expensive, he did not seem to account for this or the gap in pay that persists between genders when he made this judgment. Would salespersons like Billie be better at persuading women if he approached them with less gendered assumptions? There are numerous examples in this chapter in which the sales associate draws conclusions about the customer that might inhibit them from attributing fluctuations in sales to their own behavior. However, there are also market conditions that are not well accounted for in the commission structures. Sales associates cannot possibly sell to people who do not come in the store (in those relevant retail outlets).

7

Electronics

In this chapter, we explore the commissions of those who work in phone stores, sell or rent electronic games, sell computers, sell audio equipment, sell corporate phone systems, and work in electronics stores. Most salespeople who sell electronic goods are grouped together with other retail salespersons, for which there are an estimated 1,836,000 workers making an average of $31,000 annually. The other relevant occupational category is sales representatives (services), for which there are 528,000 workers making an average of $56,000 annually.

Most electronic goods are sold on commission, and the commission structure is often very complex. Commissions are intended to operate as an incentive to promote sales and growth as well as facilitate the development of a sales force that is competent, efficient, and motivated. Sales staff who are not sufficiently competent in electronics, are inefficient, or unmotivated are likely to be pushed out or opt out of employment if the commission structure is well-designed. The commission system may be based on a sales quota and may include a bonus. The structure of the commission system is partially reflected in the commission rate. Commission rates may be flat, tiered, based on the draw (also referred to as a guarantee), or may even be capped. The flat commission is a predetermined, fixed portion of the transactions paid to the salesperson. For example, Max who works at a video game store in Chicago reported that he makes a flat commission of $2 on each new membership and $3 on renewals. Commission rates may be variable in some cases in which the portion is determined against attainment of a goal for a specific performance measure (usually sales volume). For example, Roman, who works at Verizon Wireless in Washington, D.C., reports that in one period he had a quota of 150 plans. His commission was multiplied by 1.3 in that period because he sold 182, exceeding his quota. The draw is basically an advance to the salesperson that is recovered against future earnings to guarantee that the salesperson earns a minimum amount of money. Draws that are not recoverable or can be forgiven are often referred to as guarantees. For example, Daniel, who works at Sound Advice/Tweeter, describes a modified draw in which one may draw upon an hourly wage. When this is done, the company may take up to half of that back in the next pay period out of an employee's commission. A cap is an agreement between the employer and sales associate that limits the amount of money an employee can make in a given period. Sometimes the amount of sales over the cap can be carried over to the next period. Caps attempt to manage the cost of the sales force, and the carryover allows for this management technique while retaining the full potential to incentivize sales. Interestingly, none of the interviewees describe caps. However, the narratives do indicate that the commission structures can change frequently and that some employers choose to lay off workers when the commissions become too costly rather than (or perhaps after) instituting caps.

The structure of the commission system is particularly weighty in a rapidly changing industry like electronics because the proportion of industry growth to sales commissions affects the nature of innovation and the sustainability of a company. Consequently, commission structures may vary based on the types of electronics a company is trying to promote, the cut of the sales force in proportion to company earnings, expected new technologies, and the sales region.

This variation in the structure of the commission system within and across the electronics industry leads to a number of interesting questions. How do sales associates experience such highly complex and variable commission structures? Are highly specialized, complex, and variable commission structures effective incentives in the electronics industry? How does the commission system relate to job satisfaction in electronics sales?

Roman has worked for the last two years at a Verizon Wireless store outside of Washington, D.C. The following narrative illustrates his perspective on commissions in the electronics industry.

I like working for Verizon. They have great benefits, and there is the potential to make a lot of money.

I have a base salary of $25,000. I also get health benefits, a 401K, and other benefits like tuition reimbursement. There are three ways that I make commissions.

1. About 60 percent of my commission comes from selling price plans. I only get a commission for new plans, plans that have lapsed, or plans

that will lapse in two months. The commission rate changes from month to month. For a $79.99 plan, the commission can range from $17 to $28. This month it is $26.10. If someone cancels their plan, they will take the commission out of my next commission check.

2. Thirty-five percent of my commission comes from enhanced services. For example, if someone signs up for text messaging, I get $8 to $10. Video streaming gets me $15, and insurance gets me $4.

3. The last 15 percent of my commission comes from accessories. I get 6 percent of the cost of the accessory.

I DO NOT get any commission for the actual phone.

Last month, my commission was $1,700. Its computation was a little complicated. I had a quota of 150 contracts, and I sold 182. Therefore, all my commissions were multiplied by 1.3. That is a big help.

Last year, I had a month in which I got $8,000 in commission. This was because I was working at a kiosk, and Verizon had a much higher commission rate because they were trying to push kiosks. I like working at the store because it is busier, although less economically rewarding. It is more fun to be busy.

There is little competition among the staff. We watch out for each other. If someone comes in to complete a sale started on the previous day, we will write it up for the person who was there the day before. We help each other out.

Andrew is a salesperson for Sprint PCS. This is his story in his own words.

I receive an hourly wage of $10.82, and my base salary comes to $22,000. My commission is based upon three factors related to quotas. If I meet my quota this month, I get an additional $1,100. The three factors are:

1. Twenty-nine new phone actualizations
2. $1,757 in accessory sales
3. Four long-distance plan sign-ups

These three factors change from month-to-month. If I do not meet the full quota, the commission is pro-rated. If I exceed the quotas, I get higher commissions on an accelerated basis. Last month I made $1,700 from commissions, and the month before that I made $2,000. Over the year, I made $19,000 in commissions.

The commission policy is nationwide.

We sometimes "cherry-pick" when a customer comes in. If a person is just buying a set of headphones, it is not as big a help for meeting the quotas. We make most of our commissions with new service actualizations.

In some stores, the salespeople work together as a team, and in others, it is more cutthroat. It really depends upon the manager and the dynamics of the sales force. My store used to work as a team. However, a new manager came in, and we added some new members to the sales force. That changed the dynamics. We are now more of a shark cage.

I like the team approach. Everyone succeeds. However, all it takes is one person not pulling their weight, and it all messes up.

We are not supposed to share commissions, but I sometimes share my quota. You are not going to use my name, right? I have some friends, like the person who trained me, whom I don't want fired. This is done under the table.

Max worked in a video game store in Chicago for seven months. This is what he had to say about commissions.

I liked working at the store. It was a very relaxed atmosphere. I got to play video games. I was pretty good at it. It was very casual.

I was paid $7.50 an hour. I got commissions from two different sources.

We sold subscriptions/memberships. These cost $20 a year and entitle the person to a 10 percent discount on used video games, sales of new games, a magazine, game demos, and the ability to play in tournaments in the store. For every membership I sold, I got $2 and for each renewal I got $3. I would typically sell about eight memberships a week.

I also got $1 for every warranty that I sold with a new system. These warranties also cost $20. They would last one year or until they were used for the first time. One woman brought a system in the day after it was sold because her son dropped it. It was easier going through us than sending it back to the factory. She had to buy an additional warranty that day because she used the one she purchased the day before.

I sold warranties to 60 to 70 percent of those buying systems. I would sell about one warranty a day during normal months.

During Christmas, I would sell fifteen warranties/systems a day. Warranties were very seasonal. Subscriptions were sold according to whether the person was buying a lot of used video games. At a certain point, it simply made sense to buy the membership and get the discount on used games. Christmas was nice. I would earn an extra $80 every two weeks.

There was no competition among the staff. We were all competent, and the manager stressed that we should all help the customer.

The commission really helped. It created a sense of urgency. I felt I needed to take control of what was going on.

*Logan sold computers for Dell Computers in Nashville, Tennessee. His job selling loans at E*trade is explored in the chapter on financial services.*

The following narrative details Logan's perspective on commissions in computer sales.

I was in the corporate division for two years. There were hundreds of people in a huge boiler room. I would get or make fifty phone calls a day. As soon as one call was done, another one would be routed my way.

I liked working at Dell. The pay was good and they had an atmosphere that encouraged growth. There were a lot of people to make friends with.

My base pay was $32,000 per year. I had a quota based on profit margin. A typical computer selling for $1,500 would have a profit margin of $200. The average profit margin on a server was higher—about 50 percent. My quota was $1.3 million in profit per month. They were making a lot off of me. If I hit my quota, I got $1,500 per month in commission. This amount would go up the longer you worked at Dell. If you hit 120 percent of your quota, you would get 180 percent of the $1,500—about $2,500. If you sold under your quota, you still got a percent of the $1,500. In a typical month, I made 130 percent of my quota. My most lucrative month was a December when I sold 180 percent of my quota.

There were a lot of other ways to make money. They wanted people to lease computers. If you were in the top quartile in leasing in your division, you would get an extra $800 for that month; the top 10 percent—extra $1,200; top half—extra $400. They did not want people to use credit cards, so you would lose some of the leasing incentive if they used credit cards.

Each month there were different incentives. They would change the metrics based upon closing rate or printer units, et cetera. Each month, the weights would change. However, the top 25 percent in sales according to that month's metrics would get an extra $750, and the top 50 percent would get an extra $250.

HP was our big competition on printers, so for every Dell printer you sold, you would get an extra $5. If you sold training and certification, you would get an extra $20. They changed these incentives each month depending upon market conditions.

In a really good month, I could make $7,000 in commission.

You could take advantage of rules. If they were pushing printers, you would negotiate a lower price for the other equipment and throw in a few "free" printers. Dell knew this was happening and allowed it because it would increase toner sales.

For a really large sale (over $20,000), you would move it up to a senior person. This would work to your benefit as you would still get full credit and would benefit if the senior salesperson finished the sale or got them to buy more.

People stole my orders all the time. You would build a quote, and when the person called back, you could steal the entire sale. There were bitter fights.

The Dell ideology said it was your problem because you did not do enough to close the sale or tell the person to call you back. You did not have the proper rapport.

There were ten to twelve of us in a team, and a manager had his incentive system based very much upon ours.

Daniel has been selling audio and visual equipment at Sound Advice/ Tweeter for almost five years. This is his story.

I love what I do. I get to see new people, and I get to solve people's wants every day. It is great to see their eyes light up when I put a package together.

Right now, I am paid $12 an hour plus commission. The hourly system will change in a few weeks. We've had a commission based on a sliding scale. This sliding scale is based upon gross profit. A typical car stereo system sells for $1,800 of which $600 is profit, and a wall TV sells for $3,500 of which $500 is profit. I get between 4 percent and 11 percent of that profit depending upon how many modifiers I sell with the products. For example, if I sell a CD player with speakers, wires, and an amplifier along with three modifiers, my commission will be 7 percent. I typically get 9 to 10 percent commissions.

In a typical week, I make $300 in commission. My best week was around Christmas when I made $1,800.

We can share commissions. They can be split 25 percent, 50 percent, or 75 percent. We have people who come in months after they first looked at an item. You have to keep records, so you know who talked to the person first and so on. Sometimes there are brief squabbles about who did what in a sale.

Most of our business is repeat buyers. I see 25 to 50 people a week of which 35 to 40 percent will close a deal.

They are about to change this system and return to a draw system. They left the draw system several years ago when they found it difficult to hire competent staff. Apparently, the numbers are down as some people got lazy relying upon their hourly wage.

Now, instead of making only an 11 percent commission, this will go up to 18 percent, and you can get another 6 percent by making a bonus. The bonus is dependent upon selling certain percentages of items such as power wire, extended warranties, et cetera, so if your commission is $1,000, you can get an additional $60 bonus by hitting your figures.

The draw is a modified draw. If you draw upon an hourly wage, they will take up to half of that back in the next pay period out of your commission, so if you get $500 in salary, they might take up to $250 out the next pay period. They are not going to take it completely away from you.

Lorenzo worked part time for three years at Circuit City in a mall in Michigan. Circuit City liquidated in 2009. This is what he had to say about commissions prior to the liquidation of Circuit City.

During my time there, the system changed from commission-based to hourly-based. While the system was commission-based, there was a base pay which was actually a subsidy. If you received compensation from the base pay one month, it would be deduced the next month. Most people earned above their quota, and their pay was not based on the base. I never saw it.

I received a commission based on every item that I sold. I sold electronics. My commission was based on the markup. A computer for $1,000 had a low markup, and I might only get $50 to $100. Accessories like head phones had higher markup. You would make little on a printer but would make $15 for a $50 ink cartridge. You made a lot from cell phones. A new phone with actualization might get me $80 to $90 irrespective of the cost of the phone. I made more money with the extra services that I would push—text messaging, et cetera. I made the most with extended service plans which were pure markup.

We never knew the formulas behind the markups.

On a big month, I would earn $900 in two weeks, working thirty hours per week. This would be during Christmas when I was on break. During the school year, I worked weekends and never put in more than twenty hours a week. I averaged $135 to $160 every two weeks.

There was a lot of competition among the workforce. The system was "meet and greet." Whoever greeted the person first and gave them some help would take the commission. We each worked in a single area of responsibility. If I got help from another associate, I could split the commission in the computer. Every once in a while I would get angry with someone else for taking a sale. Customers don't always go back to the person they got their information from. There is a whole culture to commission sales.

At one point the whole company reorganized to an hourly wage. Your hourly wage was dependent upon your history of commissions. I got $9 an hour. Some people would have received $22 an hour. However, this was too high, so Circuit City fired them after giving them a good severance package. They basically fired their best employees.

I prefer the hourly wage system. It is not as high stress or cutthroat. They still compare you with the other associates, but there are now other ways to measure your performance. The hourly wage does discourage competition to a degree. Now they promote you to different positions: product specialist, leader, etc., instead of just based upon salary.

We were previously not paid for stocking. There were other people paid by the hour. When we were asked to stock, we would try to avoid it. It did not help us on our commissions. Now we punch in a clock, and we are there on time.

Samuel has been working at a Radio Shack in Delaware for fifteen years. He shared the following story about commissions in the electronics industry.

I love it. The people are friendly, and I have fun solving problems. We have a lot of little old ladies who need help, and we get together and solve it. It's fun.

I get paid $8 an hour. The commission structure is a puzzle to me. It is very nebulous, and I don't fully understand it. I have to sell over $100 an hour to get a commission, and then I get 5 percent. I think each hour starts the clock over, so if I sell $10 one hour and $110 the next hour, I still get a commission. However, I am not sure about this. On average, I make $25 a day in commission. On my best day, I made $500 in commission.

Christmas is great. I can make a couple thousand a week in commissions. Black Friday (the day after Thanksgiving) is unbelievable. We will have a couple hundred people waiting to get in at 8 am. We will advertise that we have ten DVD players at $10. There is quite a rush.

There are also some special "spiffs." For every cell phone activation, I get $35, and I get this if they come in and renew. I usually sell about sixty cell phones a month. It is a mystery to me that we still sell so many cell phones. You would think everyone would have one. However, a lot of people get mad at their carrier and switch. I also get $25 extra for each Dish TV.

There is some competition among the staff. You can work with someone on a Saturday for two hours and they come back the next day to make the purchase. Someone might steal your sale. There might be words exchanged but no fisticuffs. We all get along pretty well. We cannot share commissions.

Sean is a salesman for a company that manufacturers network wiring. This is his story.

I sell Cat5, Cat6, fiber optic, and so on. I've been with this company about a year, but I've been in the business for thirteen years. I've been through the ups and the downs. The company I work for is fabulous, but I might want to change industries.

My salary is $85,000 per year. My commission is based 70 percent upon the group I am in and 30 percent upon my own individual goals.

There are six of us in our group, and we are responsible for a given territory. It is a great group. If the group meets its goal, I get an additional 20 percent of my salary. So, if our goal is $5 million in sales and we meet that, I would get $17,000 ($85,000 x .20). Last year we actually got 25 percent, as we exceeded our goals. The goal goes up every year.

I also met my personal goal. This added 5 percent onto my salary. The personal goal is based upon number of visits you make, your own sales, and so on.

To be honest, the system is a pain in the ass. I really don't fully understand the criteria. The system is too complex.

We sell mostly to contractors. Orders can range from $1,000 to $500,000. I don't make too many cold calls. Mostly it comes from referrals.

Our commission is paid out quarterly. We also have profit sharing. Last year the company put $4,000 into my 401K from the profit sharing. I have no idea how they arrived at that number.

Please don't send the $10.

The next set of stories concerns sales of Verizon services. The referrals all came from the same source, and the stories highlight how specialized, segmented, and complex a commission structure can be in electronics sales. The following respondents work for Verizon in various capacities, demonstrating the dynamics of a commission system from within a very large organization.

Sarah is an inside sales representative at Verizon. This is what she had to say about the commission system.

I sell to already existing accounts of customers who have under $100,000 a year in sales and service. These could be radio stations or sports teams. Restaurants are too small, and hospitals are too big. I have 300 to 400 customers.

My base salary is $40,000 per year. I also have a goal set which if I meet will allow me to make $25,000 a year in commission. The goal is based upon three different buckets: new services (50 percent), new equipment (20 percent), and renewals (30 percent). One of my buckets is new services of $28,000 per year. For each percentage I get toward that goal, I get $150 commission. The system is very complicated as I have different buckets for each account.

Last year I got 90 percent of the $25,000. Once I sell over the objective, I start getting 1.5 times the commission rate, and if I reach double my objective, I start getting double the commission rate.

I deal with already existing accounts. I make regular calls. For example, hurricane season is about to begin in Florida, and I am calling my customers. I tell them that I am your account manager and ask whether they have a disaster plan in place. If not, I tell them about the several plans we have available. At the same time, I might ask who their long-distance carrier is, et cetera.

My primary accounts I call twice a month. These are in the $100,000 a year range and require handholding. I have secondary accounts that I call monthly or every couple of months. There are even smaller accounts that I call once or twice a year. I need to stay in contact with my customers.

I like the fact that I have accounts tied to me. I get paid if they renew automatically or if they order a new set of phones from someone else. I don't always understand the system well, but it works. I have the potential to make a lot of money if I put in the work.

Francis is a corporate account manager for Verizon. She shared the following story.

I've been at Verizon for two and a half years, but I've been doing sales for seventeen years. I can't imagine taking home a paycheck without my performance being part of it. I work with very large corporations that bill $4 to $5 million per year. I have eight large accounts. My base salary is $73,000.

There is a new system to compute my commission. The system has three buckets:

1. network services (data and voice);
2. physical equipment; and
3. the amount of growth over the previous year.

I can't just lose $200,000 from one part of the service and make it up with $200,000 in another part. The weights of these three buckets are 40 percent, 40 percent, and 20 percent, respectively. I have a yearly quota for all three. My monthly check looks at the percent progress toward all three. For example, I am supposed to bring in an additional $25,000 in revenue each month. If I do that, I get $4,000 from that bucket for the month. Last year, I made $57,000 in commissions.

The system is very complicated, and I don't pay much attention to it. I don't worry about the details. If they tell me there is a special on a certain type of service that month, I won't push it unless it makes sense for the client.

For one of the clients, I have my own office on site. I talk to my other clients at least once a week.

I like my job. It is all about quality control. You get out what you put in. The major problem is that I get taxed at a higher rate, but it is close to owning your own business while you get to use someone else's resources.

Bernard processes contracts for Verizon and shared this story.

I do support work for people who sell telecommunication services to government and education accounts. We put in T1s, voice to data, VOIP, et cetera. I process the contracts. I put them in our database, deal with billing problems, and make sure the work orders go to the right people. I do more administrative work.

I like what I do. It is not boring. It is always a challenge. The recent merger of MCI and Verizon created lots of headaches.

My salary is $60,000 per year. I also get a commission based upon the work of the salespeople. I get 20 percent of the total commission of my work-group or a minimum of $500. There are four salespeople in my group. If their combined commission is $10,000 per quarter, I would get $2,500. In a typical quarter, I get $1,000 to $1,500 in commission.

My commission is really based on their work and not my work. They get a bigger chunk, and I get a smaller chunk.

Howard sells telecommunications equipment to the federal government. The following narrative reflects his responses during the interview.

The company I work for is a smaller version of Verizon. I sell voice services, Internet access, enterprise communications, WANs, LANs, ISPs, VOIPs, and video conferencing. I have been at this company for three years, but I have been in the industry for twenty years. Previously, I did similar work for AT&T. I like the job because it is not a 9-to-5 job. I have an interest in technology, and it is fun to be cutting-edge. It is a fascinating process dealing with the government. The days go quickly.

A person in my position makes $70,000 to $90,000. I make a commission on all sales. The commission rate varies between 5 and 10 percent depending upon the product. Data products such as WANs and LANs are at the higher end because the profit margin is greater.

A typical deal might be for $500,000 over three years. I would get my commission for the first four to six months of billing, so an 8 percent commission for six months would be about $6,700. The same principles apply for sales to the private sector.

I do mostly new sales. I often do the equivalent of cold calls. I work with partners in other companies who sell complementary products who refer me. I subscribe to a variety of relevant journals and data services and read the RFPs. In essence, the government agency that I am calling has a problem, and I try to offer a solution.

In an average month, I make forty calls a month, and these result in five to six meetings. I try to get four contracts a year. A typical contract is for $500,000 but can range into the millions.

Within the company, we have established groups, and we all get along.

We have a bonus program in addition to the commission. If I meet my quota, I get an additional $1,000 per quarter.

The commission structure changes each year. Typically, this is not in your favor. You have to look at your commission statement each month. In about half the months, there is an error. Occasionally I get overpaid. I tell them that as well because it will eventually be found.

The commission structure is far too complex. I think the company designs it that way. It differs deal by deal. Commissions are supposed to be an incentive, but it's important to remember that the company has its own goals.

The narratives in this chapter demonstrate a number of important aspects of commission systems. The computation of commissions in the electronics industry is often very complicated. Yet, electronics sales associates tend to have an advanced understanding of the commission structure, even when it changes regularly. In fact, the commissions function as incentives to promote specialized sales. They also influence the behavior of the sales staff and moderate the interactions between the sales staff and customers. For example, the "cherry-pick[ing]" noted by Andrew is an example of how the incentive structure impacts which customers the sales staff are more likely to engage and the kind of service the sales staff provides certain customers.

There are as well some sales associates in electronics who are puzzled by some aspects of the commission structure. In those instances in which the sales associate does not clearly understand a given aspect of the commission structure, they appear to calculate a general average that they use to determine if the pay is adequate. A commission system that is perceived as unnecessarily complex may foster mistrust and has the potential to impact job satisfaction. Sales associates do tend to tailor their behavior very specifically the more the commission system is transparent.

It also appears that when the sales staff has a strong working knowledge of the commission system, they may develop informal arrangements that foster the type of work environment that minimizes competition among the sales force. For example, Roman stated that at the Verizon store where he works they "watch out for each other" by assigning sales to the salesperson who worked with a customer the previous day when the customer returns to complete a sale the next day. Andrew pointed out that commission sharing against policy occurs between members of the sales associates so that people "work together as a team."

Additionally, the narratives in this chapter validate the effectiveness of a well-structured commission system in conjunction with a skilled manager. The story shared by Max who sold video games illustrates this point. Max described how the manager hired competent sales associates, oriented the sales staff toward customer service, and maintained a work environment that minimized hostility; while the commissions served to foster a sense of "urgency."

8

Auto Parts, Sales, and Service

The Census Bureau does not have a special code for car salespersons, motorcycle salespersons, or auto parts and services salespersons. They are coded as retail salespersons (1,836,000; $32,000). Car salespersons, and particularly used car salespersons, have a reputation for being dishonest in their search for commissions. In repeated surveys by Gallup, car salespersons are the lowest rated of twenty occupations for their honesty. Many people find the process of car buying particularly distasteful. One may reasonably think that a system such as *Checkbook Magazine*'s suggestions for getting e-mail quotes from car dealers might make the process of buying a car more efficient. Customers are still likely to contend with last-minute sales pitches for extended warranties, Scotchgarding, maintenance packages, and so on. Completing a car purchase in under a few hours is a tremendous feat. What's in it for the sales associate? How do sales associates experience this process? What is the nature of the commission structure in the automotive industry that contributes to a sales atmosphere that most of us dislike?

Andrew has been selling cars for over forty years. The following narrative details his perspective on the commission system.

I work for an automotive group which has forty-five dealerships in the mid-Atlantic area. I can sell cars from any of the forty-five dealerships. People will go to me instead of the actual dealer because they either know me or have been referred by someone. I will find the car they are looking for usually within our own organization.

My salary is 100 percent commission. I get between 25 percent and 30 percent of the gross profit from the sale. The same process works for used cars as well as new cars. I can't tell you what an average gross profit is. It depends upon the model, make, year, and style. It is up to the salesperson to try to make as high a gross margin as possible. It is also hard to figure out with dealer rebates, et cetera. Some cars have a gross margin of $500, and others might be $2,000 to $3,000. Usually a Lexus or Mercedes has a higher gross margin than a Toyota or Chevy, but even the luxury cars can have low margins when they are not in demand.

I talk to about five to ten people a week that come into our showroom. I average selling one to three cars a week. I also make money from selling extended warranties for which I usually get a flat rate of $25 to $50. I also usually get a flat rate for after market add-ons such as chrome wheels, stripes, and floor mats. Because I deal with so many dealers, the amount really varies and is sometimes a percentage.

I also get money from different sales promotions. A dealer may say, "Sell ten or more of these cars and you get an additional $50." On the other hand, if they are trying to get rid of cars, they will sell them at invoice (no gross margin) and have a minimum commission of say $50 or $100.

Hector has been selling Hondas in the Washington, D.C., area for fifteen years. This is his story.

I like selling cars. I like the challenge. I control my own income. I earn 100 percent commission. There are five levels of the commission structure. If you sell 1 to 8 cars per month, you get 20 percent of the gross profit. The highest level is 23 or more cars per month. At this level, I would get 35 percent of the gross profit. Last month I sold 25 cars.

The typical profit margin on a popular car like the Civic Hybrid is about $1,100. For cars that are not selling well, the profit margin will be lower. Some types of Accords are not selling well, and there is a minimum $50 incentive for any car that you sell.

There are also a variety of monthly bonus programs. If you sell five cars in a week, you would get $500; two cars in a week, you would get $200. In addition, the person who sold the most units would get $300.

I get a little incentive for financing. I get 1 percent. If the person is financing $15,000 I get $150. I get no commission for the accessories.

The sales staff gets along with one another. There is no stealing of sales. If someone does a test drive with me but comes in a month later and buys the car from another agent, I can go to the manager and get half of the deal.

Dorothy has had several jobs involving commissions. Her experiences selling insurance and selling appliances at Sears are included elsewhere in this volume. The following narrative details Dorothy's experience with commissions for auto sales.

I have been selling Volvos for the last three months. I love it. The dealership is like a family. We are all close. It is not competitive here. We are a team. It really is a family business.

We use the draw system. I get a minimum of $800 every two weeks.

For each car that I sell, I get a minimum commission of $100. For the first ten cars that I sell per month, I get 24 percent of the profit margin; between 11 and 14 cars, I get 27 percent. Anything over 14 cars, I get 30 percent. Sometimes there is no profit on a car, and you are just getting the minimum. A lot of it depends on what is going on at Volvo and how long the car has been on the lot. On a typical sedan, I would make $250 in the sale. We do best on used cars.

I also get a small amount for the financing. I would get less than $100, probably closer to $20.

Accessories are odd. I might actually lose on accessories because it would be rolled into the total cost. If I sell the accessory (like a $2,000 backseat) after the sale, I might get 10 percent.

We also have a bonus system. If I sell ten units in a month, I get $1,000. There are other incentives they will use each month. I sold eight units last month, which is pretty good for a newbie.

There is no stealing among the sales staff. It would not be tolerated. If someone sold nine units each month, although this is not supposed to happen, someone might give me the tenth unit, so I could get the bonus. We help each other out.

Jonathan sold cars for a Toyota dealer for three months. He now does graphic design. This is what Jonathan had to say about the commission system in car sales.

I hated that job so much that I left. I've been a car nut all my life. I really love BMWs and owned over ten of them. I used to instruct people how to drive at high speed. I had very high expectations when I started the job. No one cared about the cars. All they wanted to know was what color they could get and how much would it cost them per month. The salespeople did not know cars. I once asked the used car manager if I could borrow some tools to take a license plate off. He said, "My wife has more tools than I do." No one talked about cars.

I had a $250-a-week basic draw in case I did not sell enough cars. Our commission was based upon the profit the dealer made on the car. If I sold 1 to 10 cars, I would get 15 percent of the profit; 11 to 18 cars—25 percent; 19 to 25—30 percent; and over 40 cars—40 percent.

We sold Prius at list—no negotiation. I would get $400 per car sold. In my last month, I sold fifteen new cars and two used cars. The same percentage worked for used cars. However, if we sold more than eleven used cars, our commission increased 2.5 percent.

There was also a minimum. We were guaranteed a minimum of $100 commission per car. That helped with discounted cars.

We also had a certain level called pro. If we made pro, we also got an additional $1,000 per month. To make pro, we had to sell ten new cars and two used cars. Half of the cars had to have $450 dealer packages. Half had to have $1,500 profit for the dealer. All customers who traded in used cars had to produce the title within thirty days. I had to threaten one with a lawsuit. I had to attend various classes; no money due from customers over thirty days. And no customer complaints and good scores on the surveys the customer was asked to fill out. For me, the biggest problem was getting customers to produce the titles.

I was good. I sold twelve cars in my first month. The manager couldn't believe how good I was.

Some of the other salespeople were good people. We could trade favors. If I had to sell twelve cars to make a quota, I could "buy" one off of one of them. Others were jerks. We were not supposed to sell used cars unless someone started in the new car area. However, if no one was around, I would talk to the customers. They would come over and steal my customer. Some of the other salespeople would have their table near the front door and jump out at customers. It was dog-eat-dog. I sold to a few customers who told me how much they hated the sales manager and the dealership.

Miles is a car salesman who shared the following story about commissions.

I just started selling Nissans. I spent quite a few years selling Toyotas. I liked selling Toyotas. The cars would sell themselves. There was a lot of politics at the dealership, but they treated me well.

I got a check every two weeks for $600. Once a month, I would get a commission check. The commission check would be my commission minus the $1,200 base pay. In essence, with the commission check, I would pay the base pay back.

I got $200 for every car I sold or 25 percent of the gross profit. If a car cost the dealer $15,000 and I sold it for $20,000, I would get 25 percent of $5,000. On a new Corolla, the typical gross (profit) would be $2,000 to $3,000. I got

25 percent of the profit or $200, whichever was higher. When we sold used cars, the same percentages applied. If the car cost the dealer $12,000 and they put $2,000 into servicing it, the gross would be $2,000 if I sold it for $16,000. I would get 25 percent of $2,000 ($500).

My percentage of the gross went up with more units sold. If I sold twelve to fifteen units a month, I would get 30 percent. For fifteen to twenty units per month, I would get 35 percent.

The average amount I made per car was $400. My biggest profit was $1,000 ($4,000 gross).

I also made money on accessories at the same percentage.

I also make a little on some financing issues—selling gap insurance and warranty packages. I only make commission on the financial issues if I sell more than ten cars a month.

There is a lot of competition among agents. Some you can trust, and others you cannot. They will pretend that you are not there when the customer comes in and asks for you. I don't have strong words with the other agent. I will talk to the manager who will usually solve the problem. We can split commissions. I have a partner. If he sells to one of my customers on my day off, we split the commission equally.

Things are different for year-end clearances and for cars that have been on the lot for over ninety days. The manager wants to get them off the lot, so we make $500 per unit and there is no extra commission. I really sometimes have to go the manager when a customer tries to get a low price. The manager is willing to break even for cars that have been on the lot a long time.

Selling cars is really about selling yourself. You have to be trusted and respected. If you are trusted and respected, people don't mind paying. People who try to pay at cost usually complain the most. The person who walks in with a Consumer's Report is more of a challenge, but we still make the sale.

At my new job selling Nissans, it is very comparable. My base is $100 per car, but my commission percentage is higher.

Felicia is the general manager for a used car dealership in South Carolina. This is her story in her own words.

I've been working for this dealership for nine years. I love what I do. I meet a lot of people, and I am a people person. I also get to learn about cars, and I set my own hours.

When a person is first hired, they earn a small hourly salary ($7 an hour) for the first three months. After that, they are on straight commission. They get 25 percent of the selling price of the car. It is not based at all upon net profit. They can also sell the customer extended warranties; which depend upon the type of car, but generally range between $1,200 and $2,800 for three year and five year, respectively. The salesperson gets 5 percent of the extended warranty.

There are two types of bonuses that a salesperson can get. If we can't get a car off the lot, we offer a $100 bonus. In addition, we give out holiday bonuses ranging from $200 for one year of service to $1,000 for ten years of service.

There is no fighting among the sales staff. If one person cannot close the sale, they might go to another salesperson for help. In that case, they would split the commission.

A really good salesperson can earn up to $100,000 a year.

Lance has sold motorcycles in Florida for the last five months. This is what he had to say about commissions.

We sell Japanese bikes such as Suzukis and Yamahas. I like the people who come in. They are laid back and relaxed. The owners are also good people to be around. I get paid a base salary of $200 a week and commission.

The commission is based upon the profit margin. I get 25 percent of the profit. This can go up if you sell over twenty bikes in two weeks. Only one person has done this since I started. I average selling twenty bikes a month.

A basic street bike sells for $3,000 to $10,000. The average profit on a $10,000 bike is $1,500, or 15 percent. The profit margin is closer to 10 percent for cheaper bikes.

If they really want to get rid of a bike, they will give us an extra $25, $50, or $100 for selling that bike. The manufacturers insist on sending us unpopular bikes in order to sell popular bikes.

We all get along. If you come in late one day and miss a sale you started, we can split the commission.

We get no payment for any apparel, parts, warranties, or financing. We only make commission from selling the bike.

He refused the $10 payment for participation.

Len is in the parts department at an auto dealership in Northern Virginia. This is his story.

I've been there for three years, and I like working there. The hours are not bad, and the pay is OK. Cars are my passion, and I want to be a mechanic.

I get paid $8.50 an hour. I am a team leader—second in charge. We have two types of sales—wholesale and interior. Wholesale is when someone orders the part from elsewhere. I get 2 percent commission. If the part is used internally at our dealership, I get 1 percent. I am not really sure how the commission structure works other than that.

I get $1,000 to $1,500 every two weeks for my commission work. It is OK. Sometimes I get $700, and that is a little rough.

Karl has been a service manager for a foreign car dealership for six years. The following narrative details his perspective on commissions in the auto industry.

I love it. I am good at it. I write up customer tickets, send the car to the shop, call the customers about issues, and oversee the service of the car.

On average, I see twenty to thirty customers per day. There is one other service manager. We are both on salary and commission. Our base salary is $1,800 a month. We also split 2 percent of the total business that the shop generates. In an average month, we generate $300,000 to $380,000 of business [note: 2 percent of $300,000 is $6,000]. We split our 2 percent evenly, and we get along very well.

It was a little bizarre changing us over from straight salary. Our pay stayed about the same. There is no real selling involved, so what was the point? There is no need to twist arms with customers. If we tell someone they need a brake job, they go along.

Our boss, who is the parts and service director of several dealerships, is paid based upon both salary and a percent of the profit margin.

The trend prevalent in the narratives of those who receive commissions in the automotive industry is variability. The common element of commission systems in auto sales and services is that commission structures appear to vary from business to business. Another point worth mentioning with respect to commissions in the auto industry is how vulnerable sales associates who make 100 percent commissions are when auto sales go down. Skilled salespersons in this industry generally have a tremendous earning potential when the economy is strong, but their aggressive tactics may have a lot to do with how much they are likely to lose if they don't make sales.

9

Miscellaneous

There are a number of jobs for which people may be compensated by commission. This chapter explores the commission system from the perspective of people who receive commissions for their work selling various products and services, including health club memberships, tanning packages, sales representatives, photography, advertising, wholesale goods, and legal services. People who sell health club and tanning memberships (as well as moving company estimators) are categorized by the Census Bureau as "sales representatives, services, all others," a category that includes 528,000 workers with an average annual income of $57,000. There were 85,000 photographers in the United States with average annual earnings of $39,000 in 2008. People who sell publications and books are considered "sales representatives, wholesale and manufacturing," a category that includes 1,286,000 workers with an average annual income of $61,000. There are 185,000 advertising sales agents earning an average of $52,000 per year, 50,000 advertising and promotion managers earning approximately $61,000, and there are 837,000 attorneys in the United States earning an average of $114,000 annually. Comparing the stories of a number of respondents across these miscellaneous job categories reveals a bit about how commissions function broadly as an incentive.

Gail has been working at a tanning salon in Virginia for the past two years. This is her story.

I am off to college next year. I do not like this job. The other staff members get in my way and try to steal my commissions. They will do almost anything to steal. We are not paid enough.

My job consists of selling memberships and lotions and cleaning the tanning booths. Sometimes I will be sent back to clean, so someone can steal a customer I am talking to. I am sick of the people that I work with.

I just got a raise to $7.25 an hour. I was making $6.25 and threatened to quit, so they raised my rate.

We have several different membership levels. Twenty-nine dollars and ninety-nine cents per month is the base membership, and if I sell that, I get $5. The rates go up to $79.95 for the diamond membership, for which I get $15. The higher the membership level, the better tanning beds that you can use. The basic bed has UV rays. The next nicest is UVA rays, and it goes up to a misting tan which is sort of a spray-on that lasts four days. I only get paid for the initial membership fee.

I also sell lotions. A $100 bottle of lotion will net me $10. Other lotions will net me $5 or $6.

I get my commission check once a month, and it is usually $100 to $200. I only work part time—perhaps fifteen hours a week. Some people who work full time and are more aggressive get checks of over $1,000. On some Sundays, I can make $100. February through June are our busy months.

At the end of the interview, Gail referred her friend who was at her house at the time and works for her salon's big competitor. The competitor salon has a very different commission structure. Kitty works at a tanning salon in Northern Virginia. She is close friends with Gail who works at a competing salon. Kitty shared the following story.

We are big competitors with the other salon. I have been here for a year. I really like working there. I get paid well. I like the girls I work with, and it is a good job for a high school student because I can do a lot of studying. I am off to college next year. I get paid $10.50 an hour.

We get $5 for each membership that we sell. For $20 a month, a person has the right to use the basic tanning bed. People get upgrades by buying upgrade packages. Ten upgrade tickets cost $60.

They just changed the commission system. It used to be that we got 3 percent of all sales as well as the membership fee of $5. Now, we get the 3 percent only if we sell the equivalent of $8 for each person that we try to sell to. It is very complicated. I still get my $5 per membership.

In a typical month, I get $300 to $400 in commissions for twenty-five hours of work. I make more per hour than my friend and more in commissions.

People try to steal my commissions. However, there are not as many people working at the salon, so we are closer friends.

We don't get any tips. We are called "tanning consultants."

Lauren has been selling memberships to a health and fitness club in Maryland for the past nine months. This is what she had to say about commissions.

I like my job. There is a lot of flexibility. I meet a lot of people, and it is challenging. I get a base salary of $600 every two weeks.

Memberships in the spa go for $600 a year or $1,000 for two years. I get 10 percent of any down payment and 5 percent of the remaining gross. If clients renew, I get 4 percent of the renewal payment. About 50-60 percent of members renew their membership. If they continue month-to-month, I do not get any commission. In an average week, I show the club to 20 to 25 people, and about half of them join. I get about $1,200 in commission every two weeks.

We try some outreach via corporate memberships and open houses, but most of our new members simply call and come in. People are more likely to join if they are motivated and have goals they wish to accomplish.

We also get bonuses if we meet our quota. My quota is 25 to 30 memberships per month, and I get $200 a month for this. We also have team bonuses of 50 to 60 memberships, and I get another $200 for this.

There are some other commissions that I make: personal training packages which sell for $400 to $600, kids' karate lessons, and so on. I get 5-10 percent for these as well.

Ethan is an accounts executive for a pro sports team in the Northeast and shared the following story regarding commissions.

I've been working for this sports team for ten years, and I like it a lot. I believe in the sport, and I am happy to help it grow. The team has a vision to which I contribute.

I have a base salary of $35,000 per year which helps me in the off season. My commission kicks in after my first $120,000 in sales. I get 5-10 percent. I get people to buy season tickets, corporate group purchases, birthday parties, and tickets in general. I will probably have $700,000 in ticket sales this year.

I get 10 percent for new season tickets and 7 percent for renewals. We are having a special game next month, and any tickets that I sell will get me 5 percent. If someone orders tickets online, the computer will know from their name and/or e-mail address that they are my client, and I will get credit.

I also get $1 to $5 per person for catering that is ordered. We have several bonus plans which net me a couple of thousand per year. This is based upon reaching quotas for different categories such as group sales, renewals, and so on.

We all get along in the office. If I get a call for someone else's account, the other person will get credit.

Rachael owns an art store in the D.C. area. This is her story in her own words.

I took over a year ago but kept the same consignment structure that had been in existence for over twenty years. We sell jewelry, glass, pottery, and so on. The consignment structure is very straightforward. I mark the item at double the cost the artist wants to sell plus one dollar. The extra dollar is for the cost of wrapping. If the artist wants to sell the item for $20, I price it at $41.

If there is a sale, I eat the difference. The artist would always get the $20 in the hypothetical example. If the item breaks, I pay.

The merchandise is owned by the artist. If it is not selling, they can take it back whenever they want. They usually keep it in the store. It is rare that I decide to take stuff off the shelf.

When the item sells, I keep the money for at least two weeks until the return period is over. If someone still returns it, I keep it, and it is my property to sell.

I never go out looking. The artists come to the store.

Most of the items in the store are nonconsignment. I go to shows, et cetera. I buy the item and usually can make more money from it.

Prices are going up because of energy costs. It costs a lot to heat the kilns, and jewelry prices are also going up because there is more demand for raw materials.

Don't send money. Give it to a charity.

Micky is a photographer with many sources of income from that profession. The following narratives detail his responses regarding commissions.

I do individual portraits. They usually go for $300 to $500. The amount depends upon how it is printed.

At events and weddings everyone else gets tipped. I never get tipped. I get paid for my time. I charge $2,000 for a five-hour package.

My photos get shown at galleries. A matted print might sell for $400 to $600. I split fifty-fifty with the gallery.

Working for magazines can be very complicated. They will pay $400 to $1,000 per day, and they will pay for pages they use. "Time Magazine" will pay $2,000 to $3,000 for a cover. The amount you get is determined by the size of the magazine, whether it is public or corporate, the size of the photo (full versus quarter page, etc), inside or outside, et cetera.

Often a magazine will see your photo elsewhere and will approach you. A quarter page photo will go for at least $200. It is a very complicated structure. "Time Magazine" wants to pay you less because they consider themselves prestigious.

I make much more in corporate or in advertising. If I am covering a board meeting or other such assignment, they will pay me a day rate of $1,000 to $4,000 per day, and often that will be for twenty days. The average is $2,500 per day.

A lot of my images go to a stock agency. They have images of beautiful girls or sunsets in Hawaii, et cetera. We used to split fifty-fifty. Now they are getting 60 percent. The sales cost really varies. If used in a textbook, you might get $50. My biggest sale was of a dessert image for a coffee machine that sold for $15,000. The average is $150 to $200. What you want to do is have the same image sold many times.

There are also sales for editorial purposes. This would be a topical photo – maybe of a murder scene, et cetera. I would contact press agencies such as Reuters or CNN or AP and try to sell it or try to sell it through an agency. If an agency distributes it, they get 50 percent.

Photography is a dying profession. It is harder and harder to make a living.

Richard has been a salesperson for an academic publisher for the last two years and shared the following story.

I like what I do. I was a political science major in college, so I get to keep up with the published works in political science. We also have a very friendly work environment.

I cover a three state region. In an average week, I see twenty to twenty-five professors a week. I show them what books we have that they could adopt and arrange to send out review copies. About a quarter of these meetings result in some type of success—a book gets ordered.

I make $45,000 a year in base salary plus commission. The commission is based upon the amount of sales in my area over $500,000. For every $10,000 over that, I get 1 percent, so if my region sells $600,000 in books, I get a $10,000 bonus. Last year I made $9,000 in bonus in the last six months of the year. The floor ($500,000) is very small. They really want to give you encouragement.

I also get a small fee if I bring in new authors. I don't know how much I get by bringing in new authors.

Bonnie purchases textbooks from professors which are later sold as used books. Bonnie was also interviewed regarding the bonus structure at Arbitron. This is what she had to say about commissions for trading in used books.

I've been doing this for three years, and it has its ups-and-downs. More people are becoming book buyers, so the competition is increasing. Furthermore, the publishers are giving out less examination books to professors.

I am an independent contractor. Each month, I download the list of books onto my computer (about the size of a small book). The attached scanner tells me how much to buy the book for. For the typical book that retails for $100, I will pay 25 percent ($25). The company I work for will give me 50 percent of the $25 as my commission. So, I would get my $25 back plus $12.50. There are some books that will pay more or less than this amount given supply and demand. The wholesaler who gave me $37.50 ($25 + $12.50), will in turn will try to sell it for double ($75). If it is sold in a bookstore, there will be an additional markup.

Some book buyers will try to give the professor much less that the 25 percent. So, for a $100 book, they might offer $15 and pocket the $10 difference. I prefer to pay the full 25 percent and make it up on volume. It is easy to change the computer setting so that it shows the price based upon 15 percent instead of 25 percent.

My sales really vary. The summer is very slow. For a very good week, I put in twenty hours and make $4,000 a month. There are few months that are this good. I know one person who makes $100,000+ and puts in very few hours. She has been doing it for twenty-five years and has a very loyal following. She goes to small colleges in the Midwest once a year. People know she is coming, and she has tremendous volume. You could not start something like that now.

I don't keep very good records. I get enough to pay my bills. If I am below in my payments, I will try a little harder. I am more leisure-oriented. I am also going to graduate school.

Most professors appear to be honest. Very few seem to ask for review copies of books simply to resell them.

Rick worked for nine months selling business executives education packages. Rick's jobs as a server at an Italian restaurant in Annapolis and selling beer and food at Washington Redskins football games are included in the companion volume on tipping norms. The following narrative reflects Rick's perspective on commissions.

I set up meetings and help to sell memberships in education packages. It is complex to describe. The job was all right. It was annoying with a lot of people hanging up on you. I felt like a telemarketer. I am now doing research for this firm.

I was paid $33,000 a year in base salary. I tried to set up meetings with business executives. The salespeople would meet with the people and try to sell them a membership. The membership entitled them the right to go to educational programs and make requests for research. The basic membership was $30,000 per firm.

I made $8,000 to $10,000 extra per year for two different reasons. If I set up more than twenty-five meetings per month, I made a $1,000 bonus for that month. Twice a year I was also given a commission check based on the sales of the memberships. I got ½ of 1 percent. I would get $150 on a $30,000 membership. Most of my extra pay came from the first source (setting up meetings).

A lot of people who work on commission also work on tips. Many of us have had several such jobs.

Abdul works for a moving company. He is both an estimator and a driver/ mover. His perspective on tipping is included in the companion volume. The following narrative details Abdul's perspective on commissions.

I'm an estimator for a large moving company. I make $50 for every estimate that I make. I am also on commission. I make 6 percent for all jobs that are sold. The typical single family move would cost $2,000 to $3,000. I get 6 percent of that ($120 to $180). I do not get paid a salary or any hourly wage. I work strictly on commission.

Debra has worked for the past year selling airtime at an affiliate of Fox TV. This is her story.

I like the kind of work that I do, but I don't like the station I work for. The work is rewarding. The harder I work, the more money I make. I also enjoy the fact that each day is different. However, the present station that I work for does not have integrity. I worked for ten years at an ABC affiliate, and there the clients came first. At the Fox affiliate, there is little integrity. All they are concerned about is the bottom line. At the previous station, I could work on community issues. Here, they tell me to stop being concerned with community issues and to be more concerned with the bottom line.

The bad reputation of this affiliate follows you. I am looking for another place to work. If you sell a $5,000 ad, they will kick it out if one of their big advertisers wants the time. As I said, they don't have integrity.

The commission structure is a little bizarre. I get a base salary of around $100,000. I am supposed to get 2 percent commission on sales over my projection. However, they take this back if the commission goes above my base salary. I actually get to keep very little of the commission. I do get 7 percent on new business. New business is defined as clients who have not advertised with us in the past. I came up with two new clients in the past six months.

A thirty-second commercial for prime time will go for $8,000 to $10,000. If it is with a top show like *American Idol*, that thirty seconds might cost $80,000. For a show with bad ratings, a thirty-second ad might only sell for $3,000.

At the ABC affiliate, I had a base salary of $20,000. Most ads came in via an agency. In those cases, they got a 15 percent discount, and I got a 2.5 percent commission. There was no ceiling like at Fox. I also got 10 percent on any new business, and my commission would be 4 percent (instead of 2.5 percent) on management-designated accounts that took a lot of work. In a good year, I could make $250,000 a year.

There are a variety of ways that I drum up business. I watch the other stations and look at the newspapers to see who is advertising. I will call them up. I do a lot of networking. About half of my contacts result from me calling the person. The other half of my contacts result from their calling me or my station.

There is a lot of "feast or famine" in this business. You can make $20,000 in one month and $2,000 the next. If the account goes from local to national, you can lose it all. The job used to be more fun and more glamorous. Some of your clients come and go while others stay forever.

Please don't send the $10.

Meghan sells advertising for a small magazine in the Southeast. This is her story.

I've been selling advertising for twenty years. I must like it if I've been doing it for twenty years. I like meeting people, and I like writing my own paycheck.

I get a salary of $1,000 a week, and I get 15 percent commission. My commission salary fluctuates, but in the last couple of years, it has been somewhat greater than my salary.

In a typical week, I make 80 to 100 phone calls. About 2 or 3 of these phone calls results in an appointment, and maybe 1 of these results in a sale. About half my sales are new sales, and the others are renewals. A full-page advertisement goes for around $1,000, and a half-page add is around $700.

What is most important is to be really open. I am not threatening. I tell them I want to see if we can be a good fit. There is no pressure.

I have to be persistent with old clients. I call them up and try to help them in some ways. Perhaps I saw an article in a magazine that might interest them, and I tell them about it. I drop them notes. I give them movie tickets or tickets to sporting events. It is important to maintain relations.

Henry works for a large newspaper in the Northeast selling advertising. He asked that the paper not be identified. The following narrative details Henry's responses regarding commissions.

I've been working for this newspaper for two and a half years, and I like what I do. The paper is very ethical. They treat people well.

We have lower commissions than most papers and have a higher base pay. The base pay for someone starting is $55,000. After five years, the base pay is $60,000. There are two sources of additional income. The first is based upon meeting your quarterly sales goal. If you get 105 percent of your goal, you get a $2,500 bonus for the quarter. If you meet 98 percent of it, you get $500. Sixty percent of us meet our quota. A typical goal might be $4 million in accounts per quarter.

We also have a bonus system based upon a variety of different factors. Thirty percent might get this bonus per quarter, and the bonus is $1,500. So in addition to your base, you can get around $4,000 per quarter.

I don't make many cold calls. In other departments, there are more cold calls. I get calls from clients or from ad agencies. I also call my established accounts and keep them up to date about new products.

Please don't send the $10.

Edgar owns seventeen stores of a fast-food franchise. This is his story in his own words.

It is a good business. It is very stressful because it lacks closure. I like the remodeling and building of new stores because there is closure. However, the day-to-day recurrent problems are boring. I thrive on stimulation.

We have bonuses for the store managers and the managers above them. This bonus program has been in existence for twelve years. There are four different measures that affect the bonus:

1. increases in sales over last year – 20 percent
2. achieved budgeted profit – 20 percent
3. quality service and cleanliness – 50 percent
4. mystery shopping (where someone goes unannounced as a customer) – 10 percent.

There is a written assessment done every quarter. If the parent company does its own assessment, that trumps our assessment. To get the bonus for #3 or #4 above, the score must be above 90 percent. Number 3 and 4 are definitely under the control of the managers.

The bonus can be 6/10 of 1 percent of sales. We have $20 million in sales, so the bonus could be $120,000 a year or $30,000 per quarter shared across the seventeen stores and two other managers. If your store has more sales, your potential bonus will be higher.

There are seventeen store managers, a district manager, and a director of operations. On average, fifteen get a bonus each quarter. The average bonus is about 60 percent of its potential, so on average, about $1,300 is added onto the quarterly pay of a manager whose base salary is $38,500. About 13 percent can be added on as bonus.

The 6/10 of 1 percent available for bonuses is distributed as follows:

1. .20 to the district manager
2. .10 to the director of operations
3. .30 to the store manager

The district manager can add $2,200 onto his salary each quarter, and the director of operations can add $3,000 to $4,000 onto his base salary of $105,000 each quarter.

I also give our holiday bonuses to my senior staff (about twenty people) such as comptrollers, et cetera. I basically give an extra week's pay as well as $20,000 in cash. I tell them, "The cash is between you, God, and the IRS."

There are also holiday bonuses that occur at the store level that are based upon awards (highest score in mystery shopping, highest increase in sales, et cetera).

I give no bonuses to the cooks, cashiers, and other people who work at the stores.

Please give the $10 to the first homeless person that you see.

Gabriel has been a drug rep for this pharmaceutical company for eight years. In order to ensure confidentiality, we used a lot of hypothetical examples.

I've been in the industry for almost twenty years. I specialize in HIV drugs, and I like what I do because our drugs make people live longer. I visit doctors' offices, HIV clinics, and meet with social workers. I make presentations and try to educate doctors about our medications.

For people like me who specialize, our base salary is between $90,000 and $120,000, and our bonus/commission ranges from $10,000 to $30,000. For someone who specializes in oncology, the base is probably $100,000 to $130,000. For new reps, their base is around $40,000, and their commissions can range from $20,000 to $30,000. A commission and a bonus are the same thing. Some companies like to use the term bonus while others will use the term commission for the very same process.

My territory is based upon zip codes. I might have 200 doctors in my territory that I am responsible for. I am given a quota for each drug and geographic area. A typical quota for a drug like Lipitor might be $500,000 in sales per quarter for that territory. Hypothetically, that rep would get $1,200 if the quota is met. Some companies will pro-rate the quota, and others will not.

Pharmacies sell data on aggregate sales broken down by drug, zip code, and physician (confidentiality of the patient is maintained). It is from these data the company can determine whether my quota was met. If a doctor prescribes a drug in one state, and it is filled in another state, the system will credit it to where the prescription was prescribed. We occasionally share quotas if a physician has multiple offices.

The quotas are determined by a very complicated formula. For example, a new drug might be expected to increase 5 percent per year while an older drug might be expected to plateau or to fall. The formula is also affected by R&D expenses, market share, co-pays, reimbursements, and other factors. I can never negotiate the quota, and sometime I can't figure out how it was arrived at. But it is probably fair, although not perfect.

Each pharmaceutical company has several reps for each territory. One rep might specialize in HIV, and another in oncology, and another in urology. Others might be responsible for primary care. All the reps might be pushing a common drug like Viagra. This complicates the commission system.

In the last year 77,000 drug reps were laid off across the country. This was affected by the recession as well as the fact that the system was too complicated. Some companies had eight to nine reps trying to reach the same doctor (mostly for different drugs). Doctors didn't have the time for this. Instead of eight to nine reps for each company trying to reach the same doctor, today there might be three to four. The drug companies got too greedy. They hired too many reps, and the system came back to bite them.

The system also changed in January 2009 when new guidelines went into effect on what you could give doctors. Now you can give sample prescriptions and an occasional educational lunch at a modest cost ($10 to $25). We can no longer give out pens and pads or take physicians to basketball games.

Unfortunately, education for physicians is getting cut back. Many physicians rely upon the drug reps for basic education. The pharmaceuticals are also cutting back grants to universities for CME training.[1] In part, this is occurring because they don't want an appearance of having a conflict. It also occurs because the pharmaceuticals are greedy. But the pharmaceutical companies have real concerns. Companies like Pfizer are about to lose its patent for Lipitor. The costs for R&D are very high, and this somehow has to be recouped.

There is no need to send me the $10.

Danielle sells eyewear for For Eyes in the Washington, D.C., area. This is her story in her own words.

I've been with For Eyes for two years, and I like it a lot. I like the people I work with. I have a flexible schedule, and we all work together. I get paid $15.50 an hour.

Our monthly commission check comes from three sources. About a third comes from extras that are added onto the sale of the glasses. For example,

I would net a dollar for a $100 lens coating and get fifty cents if the lens is progressive. I do not get commission on the actual glasses.

Another third of the commission check is determined by sales increases for the store compared to last year, so if our monthly store sales were $10,000 last August, they might set a goal of $15,000 for this August.

The last third of the commission check comes from *not* having overtime for the store. If the store has overtime, this reduces the commission. Total wages for the store are a component. There is a trade-off. Most of us in the store are fairly experienced and have a high hourly wage. Because of our experience, we sell a lot, which increases our commission. On the other hand, our commission is reduced because we are experienced and have a high hourly wage.

In essence, two-thirds of the commission comes from how the store operates, and the other third comes from my selling extras. My monthly commission checks range from $300 to $700.

I sometimes feel pressure to push options that are not necessary. A senior citizen does not need coating for nighttime driving. I won't push it. This is a moral issue for me.

One issue is that the company does not take problems beyond our control into account. August is one of our busiest months. December is also busy. The air-conditioning system has been broken, and we lost a lot of sales because we had to close early. This is not our fault, but we will be penalized because our commission check will be reduced. It's not fair.

Eric works for a pest management company. His job working at Brooks Brothers is presented in the chapter on clothing sales. The following narrative details Eric's experiences with sales commissions in pest management.

I like working for this company. I've been here for about one year. I previously worked in retail clothes for fifteen years. I had no life on the weekend. Now that I have an eight-year-old, I wanted a job with more freedom and flexibility. I want to take my kid to football and soccer games.

We have a draw system. My draw is about $1,500 a month. I get a straight 15 percent commission. If I have to use the draw, it is subtracted from my commission in the next pay period, so I am expected to sell about $10,000 of products per month. The commission is gravy. I've not had to rely upon the draw. In a good month, I sell about $30,000 in products ($4,500 commission). I get commission for the first year's business. There is no residual for retention.

Spring and summer are fairly busy. Last winter was pretty mild, so business was also good. If it is cold, we still get business from mice and other rodents coming into the house.

We also have a bonus system. If I sell over $200,000 of products per year, I get an extra $1,000. This goes up in steps. I get about $5,000 to $7,000 per year in bonuses.

They are thinking of moving more toward a salary-based system. The business is family owned, and they are concerned about salespeople who have a tough time in the winter.

I get business from three different sources. Ten percent is self-generated. I go out into the field and put up door hangers and walk into stores. Another 10 percent comes from referrals. The remainder comes from our call center. People call the call center because of ads in the Yellow Pages, mailings, flyers, and so on. I close about half of the sales calls that I make.

Frank has been a funeral director in North Carolina for the past thirty years. This is his story.

I like what I do. God called me to do this. I enjoy helping people. I enjoy working on bodies, and I enjoy going to funerals. I am Baptist, but we will bury anyone.

Funeral costs are divided into separate categories. The cost of the grave site depends upon the area of the country. I used to have a funeral home in Harlem. In New York City, it cost me $300 to $4,000. In my area, most people purchase plots for $200 to $300 from the county. If the family uses a vault, we pay $700 and charge $1,000. I will charge $450 for opening and closing the casket. About $150 of that is profit.

Caskets can range a lot in cost. Michael Jackson's cost over $100,000. The average casket costs me $1,000 which I sell for $1,600 to $1,700. Very rarely do people buy caskets in this part of the country for more than $2,000 or $3,000.

We charge $125 to remove a body from the hospital. I have to pay a man $60, and we use a hearse that cost me $50,000. We charge $375 for the limousine, and I have to pay for a driver, gas, insurance, as well as the cost of the limousine.

I charge $550 for embalming, and the embalmer is paid $250.

If someone is cremated, I will rent the family a casket for $650. The cremation itself costs $210. I don't mark that up.

I charge $325 for use of the chapel. I have to pay the mortgage on the building, taxes, and so on.

I charge a professional fee of $1,375. This is for my time, secretarial time, licenses, fees, and maintenance of the cemetery.

A typical casket spread of flowers costs $125. I don't mark this up, although other funeral homes will mark it up.

For the average funeral, I charge $6,000, and my profit is between $1,500 and $2,000. In this state, the merchandise (casket, etc.) are not taxed; although the services are taxed.

About half the people have insurance with Aetna or another company. It is all set up in advance, and there is less stress for the family. If the funeral costs $6,000, and the family has a policy of $10,000, Aetna will pay me the $6,000, and the balance will go to the family.

If people try to negotiate, they can usually negotiate me down to $4,800. I can live with $4,000. In New York City, everyone negotiates. In Carolina, less people try to negotiate as we have more retirees in this area. They have thought through the process in advance.

The competition in my industry is an intense problem. A funeral should be sacred. Other funeral homes have gimmicks. If you call around you, they will always tell you that they are cheaper. It becomes like a shopping mall. We buy the caskets and services from the same place. I know how much it costs them. If they have a lower cost, they will use cheaper merchandise.

Every funeral is different. It is like buying shoes. Everyone has a different fit.

William sells commercial security systems in a city in the South. These systems are placed in supermarkets, banks, churches, and so on. The systems include locks, cameras, antitheft devices, and alarms. This is what William had to say about commissions.

I like what I do. I can work very hard and do very well. There is no cap on what I can make. I am one of their top sales representatives in the United States.

A typical system will sell for between $10,000 and $30,000. On top of that there are monthly management and maintenance fees that can range from $70 to $500 a month. Most businesses will lease the systems because of some tax advantages. Most churches will buy the systems as the tax advantages do not apply to them.

Large churches can be very expensive as some want remote viewing capability, sensors in every room, sensors on all the AC units on the roofs, and sensors to stop the theft of copper gutters. A large church system might cost $50,000.

I earn a base salary of $45,000 and receive commissions of between 10 percent and 15 percent depending upon my monthly quota. I do not get a residual (a percentage of maintenance fees after the first year). With a lease, I get my percent for the year up-front. Our company encourages leases, and our commission will be 2 percent higher.

I also get a yearly bonus of about $500 if I sell 115 percent of my quota. I've also won trips to Paradise Island and St. Thomas.

The major problem is leads. Almost all leads come through the company. I occasionally do some cold calling. If I get a referral, I will give the person two to three months of free monitoring.

It takes a different breed to work on commission. I used to sell automobiles. Our company also sells home security systems. It is much easier to make a sale. The typical home security salesman is expected to sell fifteen or so systems per month. But, I don't want to go to people's homes, and I make more money selling commercial. One big deal can make your quota for the month.

Thomas sold furniture. His job in a hookah lounge is included in the companion volume on tipping norms.

I sold furniture in Brooklyn for four years. It was a mom-and-pop store. I made $250 a week plus commission. For any one sale under $1,000, my commission was 2 percent. If the total sale was over $3,000, I got 3 percent. I made an average of $60 a day in commissions. My biggest day was when I made $5,500 in one day when a person refurnished her entire apartment: living room, dining room, bedroom, and kitchen.

It can get very vicious among the sales staff. The commission is supposed to go to the person who rings up the sale. Sometimes you start the discussion, but the person comes back the next day. If you can get them to put down even a dollar deposit, it is your sale. I have had some big fights. I gave in as I realized it was not worth such a big hassle over $50. The other person had a wife and kids.

Doug has worked part time at Marlo Furniture for the last fifteen years and shared the following story.

I only work weekends and holidays. I like the commission structure, and I like the flexibility. If it is a slow day, I can just leave. I am only paid commission.

For cash sales, I get 5 percent, and for credit card and finance sales I get 4.5 percent. If there is a clearance item, the commission rate is a bit higher (5.5 percent). We also have bonuses. If I sell over $20,000 of furniture in two weeks, I get a $75 bonus; over $30,000, I get a $150 bonus.

In a decent holiday weekend, I will sell $10,000 to $15,000. My commission will be around $500 to $750. My real average is $5,000 to $6,000 in sales or around $250 in commissions. I only get paid on deliveries, not sales. If the person returns the item, the commission is subtracted from my next paycheck.

We don't have strong competition among the sales staff. We essentially rotate sales. If the person comes back on another day and I am not in, the commission can be split as long as I've entered their name into the system.

I do not get any commission for opening Marlo credit lines.

Manfred sells tires and batteries at an NTB store in Pennsylvania. He is paid $7.75 an hour and makes commission. The following story reflects Manfred's experiences with the commission system.

I also get commissions. For every Michelin tire that I sell, I get $4. Therefore, for a set of four, I would get $16. If I sell the house brand tire, I get $8 a piece. I get $1.75 for batteries and $10 for an oil change. With tire alignments, I get the full price ($69.95). I don't know why so much is paid for oil changes and alignments. The stores were originally owned by Sears, and the salesmen were really unhappy about the old commission. When the stores changed management, the rates were raised.

In an average week, I make $500 to $600 in commissions and $370 in my salary.

There is a lot of competition among the salespeople. However, we understand each other. We rotate customers. There is no fighting or arguments. You know that the next customer will be yours. We trust each other.

I never share my commissions with anyone.

Commission work is up and down. You have good and bad weeks. I love working for commissions. You have something to work for. It makes you want to sell, and the work is not boring. I want to go to work to make money.

Dorothy sold appliances for Sears for four years when she went to school in Maine. Her jobs selling Volvos and going door-to-door selling insurance are also included in this volume. The following narrative details Dorothy's experiences with commissions for the sale of appliances.

It was really good money. I liked it a lot until they bought K-Mart and changed their commission structure. My job was 100 percent commission. There was a draw system of minimum wage. I always made above the draw. Their system was that if I need to use the draw, I would repay from future paychecks.

The commission depended upon the product. Low-end appliances had half of 1 percent. The higher end had 10 percent. The customer was important. I would be willing to get a lower commission because it might be best for the customer. I would not have to deal with complaints, and I would get referrals.

Some salespeople tried to steer people toward the high-commissions sales. One person was fired when he was found showing a customer the commission structure and told the consumer it was consumer ratings with a ten being the highest!

I made the equivalent of $35 per hour with the commission structure. I had health and other benefits. I had paid vacations based on my $35 per hour average.

My best month was during air-conditioning season. In Maine, people buy window units. I would just ring them up. We sold all our air conditioners in a couple days of the beginning of the hot season. I made $3,000 a week working part time. It was a good part-time college job.

The competition was a shark pit. You could be working with a customer for a week designing their kitchen, and the day they come in someone would steal your sale. Words were often exchanged. Some people were worse than others. There were alliances, and the manager usually decided that once the sale was rung up, it was final. Splitting of commission was not allowed.

A lot of that has changed. Sears changed the commission structure so that it would range between 2 and 5 percent instead of half of 1 percent and 10 percent. It might seem more fair for the customer, but the sales staff made less money and began to care less. Before the change, good salespeople always cared more about the customer than the commission rate because you did not want complaints.

I like commission work. I worked for Best Buy for two months. After two months, I was number two in the country at selling warranties. It did not affect my paycheck. It drove me nuts.

Terry just started working for a landscaping company. His work for a sporting goods store is included elsewhere in this study. The following narrative details Terry's experiences with commissions at the landscaping company.

The work pays pretty good, but it is pretty exhausting. I get paid $10 an hour. The last couple weeks I spread a lot of lime on lawns.

I get commission when I upgrade someone. If they purchase something besides what they ordered, I get 7 percent. If I spread more that $1,500 a day worth of lime, I get 7 percent of that. If they sign the invoice, I get $2. If they give me a check when I am there, I get $5. I get about $100 a week from these commissions. I get more business on Saturdays when the people are more likely to be home.

I'm not yet a technician. You have to be twenty-one. When I become a technician, I will get a salary of $400 a week plus I can make the commission discussed above. I can also make more on overtime.

Jack had a job for several years delivering ice. His work as a locksmith is included elsewhere in this study. Jack's commissions for ice delivery are discussed in the following narrative.

It was very hard work. You loaded up twenty-five tons of ice, drove it to a store, unloaded the ice, and then stacked it in the ice chests. We sold ice to convenience stores as well as supermarkets.

My salary was 100 percent based on commissions. I received no hourly wage. The commission was determined by the distance driven and the size of the store. I got between 7 percent and 14 percent of what was charged to the store. The longer the travel distance and the smaller the store, the greater my percentage.

I would clear $600 to $700 a week after taxes. We did 75 percent of our business in the summer. If I really hustled, I could do my route in six hours. I could bust my butt and be done.

I like the motivation of being the best employee you can be. I don't like to be lazy. Commissions are good for me.

Danielle has been driving a delivery truck for Frito Lay in southern Florida for the past two years. This is his story.

I deliver chips to convenience stores and supermarkets. I bring the chips into the store, rotate the product on the shelf, put the new chips up, and take back the boxes for recycling to Frito Lay. I like my job. I am not cooped up in an office all day, and I get to run around.

I am also a salesperson. I take down the orders. I try to encourage them to put up displays and to fill the shelves with new products. The job is as much sales as delivery.

I am paid hourly and by commission. I don't know the exact amounts. Some drivers can tell you to the penny what they make. I can't. I get around a 1 percent commission for most deliveries. A typical order to a store is between $800 (convenience stores) and $3,000 (Walmarts). I get a smaller commission percentage for larger stores because the volume is supposedly greater. The percentage is a little smaller when I drive the big trucks. I make three to four deliveries per day. My base salary is around $400 a week, and I get $300 to $800 a week in commission.

The commission really varies. It is very seasonal in Florida. I do much better during the tourist season and before hurricanes.

Kate sells industrial lighting to companies in southern California and shared this story about commissions.

I am a manufacturer's rep for the best lighting company in the world. I will sell a four-foot fluorescent lightbulb for $19 that Home Depot will sell for $2. We are the Rolls Royce of lightbulbs. I love my job, and I've been doing it for a year.

I'm paid straight commission. The commission is 34 percent on most items.

I go to businesses that use lights and talk to the receptionist. I ask who in the building is responsible for making decisions about buying lights. I try to joke with the receptionist. These are cold calls. If the receptionist tells me,

I call and try to make an appointment. These buildings can be strip malls or medium-size businesses. The larger companies usually won't deal with me.

When I meet with the person responsible for making the decision, I give a brief and aggressive presentation. My typical first order is for $250 to $400 in sales. The sale has to be on that day. If they say to call back, you have lost control of that customer.

The secret is repeat business. Once I've made a sale, I can get repeat business 80 to 85 percent of the time. The first year of doing this work is very hard.

I sold all lighting needs to one particular jewelry store. The total order was $700. I will not get repeat business from them for a while because our warranty is five years.

My very first sale was $1,400. I said, "Wow! How easy could this be?" That did not happen again. It was a fluke.

There is no sharing of the commissions. However, I give sales aids to the person making the decision as a thank you gift (not the receptionist). The sales aid might be a nice calculator. If they take the sales aid, you have a potential buyer. When they place orders, we give them nice thank you gifts. For example, for a $700 order we give a gift valued at $32. This might be a fishing tool, coffee maker, or pocket knife.

The company sends a trainer every two to three weeks. They will go with me to presentations I have arranged. If I match what they sell in three days, I get a double commission. The last trainer sold $1,400. If within the next three days I sell $1,400, I get a commission of 68 percent. The trainers are very helpful. I watch them.

I get my commission every Friday sent directly to my checking account. I have a weekly goal ($2,000 a week in sales). If I exceed $3,000, I get a bonus. I've not yet hit the bonus.

There is no real territorial exclusion. However, there is only one other rep in this area. My accounts are protected for one year. I got a commission on $1,300 in sales because I had already sold to that customer within the last year.

The commissions are very generous. There are no quotas. My initial investment was $300. This paid for training and samples. They will give you this $300 back when you open enough accounts. The CEO makes a big deal of giving you the check, and they wine and dine you.

Lance sells different kinds of cabinets and shared this story about commissions.

Most of the cabinets are kitchen and bath. I've been doing this for seven years, and it is a perfect fit for me. I can draw upon my experience in construction, sales, and installation. I am empathetic with the installers and can work with the contractors and everyone else. I recently became a partner in the firm.

The commissions are based upon net margins. We try to have a profit of 30 percent or higher. If you are just starting out, you might be hungry and be willing to work for a lower profit. I have an older customer base of like-minded people, so my margin can be 40 to 45 percent. We sell good quality cabinets that will have few problems, and the contractors and builders and architects that I work with are willing to pay a bit more for less headaches.

We get 9 to 11 percent of the sales price or about 33 percent of the profit. We are willing to take a smaller profit with a large condo building because the total profit will be higher.

If you need a lot of support and assistance, you get 9 percent. If you are doing most of it on your own, you can get 11 percent. It is based on how much it costs the company to employ you. We have one guy who sells $400,000 per year and gets 37 percent of the profit because he works by himself. Another guy has $700,000 a year in sales, but with that volume, he needs more as-sistance, so he gets 33 percent.

I make no calls to get business. The architects and builders know me and come to me directly or send their clients. My closure rate is 90 percent. Some-one with less experience will have a closure rate of 60 percent.

I get the job unless I've done something wrong. It is like dating. I have many long-term clients. But over time, the battles can wear you out, and you get divorced. You get tired of the old history, and someone gets tired of the other person's screw-ups. Sometimes you cut your losses.

About 25 percent of the architects or builders want a "spiff" or a cut. If the cabinet sells for $4,200 and they want $800, we will charge the customer $5,000 and pass the $800 to the architect or builder. If a private person refers me, I will send them a gift certificate to a nice restaurant for maybe $100.

Lance refused the $10 payment for his participation.

Judy is an interior designer in South Florida and sells window treatments. This is her story.

I've been doing this for ten years, and I fell into it. I am good at what I do, and because of that I can do quite well. We are a small store, and I work with two other people who own the store. We all get along. I specialize in fabrics such as drapes and cornices. I help a person choose colors, design, and so on. The owners specialize in shades, blinds, and top treatments. We do both design and sales.

I work at the store four days a week and get $150 a day. I also get a commission.

Orders can range from $1,000 to $10,000. Somewhere between 35 percent and 50 percent of that is profit. I split the profit on the fabric part of the order equally with the store. If I help sell and design other parts of the order, I might also get some type of split. That is up to the discretion of the owners.

I go out a lot on appointments. The store has been established a long time, and all our sales are by referral. If I go out on an appointment, 90 percent of the time I will get an order.

Nolan has been selling windows and doors in the Washington, D.C., area for fifteen years. This is his story.

I like what I do. I like my independence, and I control my own income. It is pretty positive.

My income is 100 percent commission. I get 30 percent of the profit made on any sale. In a typical sale, the profit is 22 to 24 percent, so for $10,000 worth of windows, I get $660 ($10,000 $\times$ .22 $\times$ .30). We also have profit sharing. Up to this year, they gave us 13 percent of our salary in one lump sum at the end of the year. This is changing to 3 percent of our salary at the end of the year and the other 10 percent will be distributed throughout the year.

There are twelve salespeople at our company. The yearly commissions range from $75,000 to $150,000.

Fifty percent of my sales come from people who call me (contractors, architects, and homeowners). The other half come from calls that I make to architects and contractors that I have had sales from in the past. There are also more traditional cold calls from information gleaned on the Internet and market share programs who give us names. I make about fifteen to twenty calls per month (both old contacts and cold). For about 75 percent of these calls, I give a bid and 25 to 35 percent of these results in a contract.

All the salespeople get along. Competition is not an issue.

Our system is different because it is based on profit of the windows and not on sales. The company tells us a suggested minimum for the sales price. Very rarely is there haggling from the customers.

Charles is a sales manager and sales representative for a company that rents construction equipment. This is his story.

I've been doing this for eleven years, and I love it. I get to work with construction guys and play with big toys. It is a lot of fun.

I get a base salary of $14,000 per year. Until recently, we got a flat 3 percent commission on rentals. My monthly commission can vary greatly. I make between $4,500 and $12,000 per month in commission.

Our biggest rental item is a cherry picker (a scissors lift). They can range from $300 per month to $10,000 per month. We will vary the price somewhat as we try to keep the gear out.

When I started, I used to make a lot of job-place calls. I would go on construction sites, ask what they are building, and who are their subcontractors. I would go to my office and call the subs and see what they needed. It is a relationship business. There is a lot of repeat business.

We used to pool our commissions. There were three sales reps, and I at first was opposed to pooling. I thought it was bull crap, but then I liked it. In good months, it killed you to pool, but in bad months it helped you out. There were less fluctuations. The company got rid of this system because some of the salespeople were on salary. They did not work as hard, so everyone went to individual commissions. This has worked well for the company as the sales reps work harder, and the market has increased.

If someone recommends someone to call, I don't give out referral fees.

Among the reps in our company, if another rep rents to someone in your territory, the rep responsible for the territory keeps the commission. If my area is Loudon and someone whose area is Fairfax takes an order from Loudon, I get the commission. What goes around comes around.

We now have a graduated scale. The bottom is 2 percent. If you rent it for its full amount, you can get 4 percent, so for a $1,000 rental that you rent for $1,000 you get 4 percent. If you rent it for $800, you get 3.5 percent and so on.

I also make commission on sales. For new equipment, I get between 10 percent and 25 percent of the gross profit. If the company is making $1,000, I get $250, if the gross margin percent is 20 percent. If the gross margin percent is 18 percent, I get 20 percent instead of 25 percent. They pay you to get more profit.

For used equipment, I get 5 percent of the gross sale price. However, the profit margin for the company must be 35 percent, or they won't allow the sale. They figure they could keep it in rental.

If you don't like to work commissions, you should not be in sales. Once you have a customer base, you get a lot of repeat business. Then, it depends upon how business is in general in your area. If one of my reps is not renting out $100,000 per month, I don't want him. Most agents rent out between $200,000 and $400,000 per month.

About 80 to 85 percent of my business is repeat business. I only get new business now when someone is coming from out of town or there is a regime change at a company.

It is really cutthroat. It used to be, "How low could you go?" It was all about price. There were a lot of bottom-feeders. We decided we would go out of business in a couple years if that continued. We decided to raise our prices. I thought we would get killed. It worked out much easier than I thought. Our customers no longer control the process. We are better than the competition, and our customers have to pay for it. We are more dependable.

There was a lot of corruption in other companies. People would buy others off with lunches, trips to Hooters, or places with less clothes, outright kickbacks, and vacations with prostitutes. One guy required that a plow be parked in his driveway during the winter, so he could snowplow; and a Cat during the summer, so he could work his garden. We would not do it, and he would not take our business.

We are big. If you make bribes, you get fired. There are a lot less independent companies now, so it is cleaner.

I will take people out to lunch, give $25 gift certificates to Home Depot for Christmas, and give out a lot of tickets to baseball, hockey, and soccer games. We can also get tickets to the NCAA Final Four. We only do this if they already have business with us.

Like all sales jobs, it depends on relationships. They have to like you.

Dave declined the $10 payment for his participation and requested that it be given to a charity he named, which was done.

John has been employed by a large law firm for fourteen years. He shared the following story regarding commissions.

I love it. I would work at half of what I make. I litigate over new technology, and it is fun. Last night I came home at 2 am because I was chasing after someone writing a brief. It was fun.

I was on the compensation committee for a couple of years. Partners get shares, and each share is worth a point. Our goal is for $5,000 in compensation for each point. The distribution is based upon a revenue stream starting January 1 of each year. For the first few months, the partners get a minimum of $100 a point, and it is not really till October that the stream really picks up. The firm actually borrows money in the first few months.

There are fourteen scales (tiers) in the firm. The lowest level is $250,000 fixed income and 20 points. This can go up to a $1 million fixed plus 225 points. It is only at the very bottom and the very top that there are fixed amounts. The lower levels have too few points and need a fixed income. The fixed amounts are used at the upper levels to attract the heavy hitters because the points are limited to 225.

In the early months of the year, the firm borrows the money. If you leave in the middle of the year, you have to pay it back. One guy is leaving now and has to pay back $800,000.

The revenue stream determines the profit per partner. We average $700,000 to $750,000 per partner. Other firms range from $400,000 to over a million.

I charge between $500 and $600 per hour. Some at our firm charge $800 an hour.

Seven and one-half to 10 percent of the revenue stream is skimmed off throughout the year. This goes into bonuses. Bonuses can range from 0 to $750,000. About 70 percent get a bonus, and the average of those who receive a bonus is $100,000.

The entire compensation system is based upon the following:

1. who originated the case;
2. who manages the case;
3. who is in charge of collections; and
4. total billable hours.

For any given case, the attorneys might decide, for example, that one attorney is responsible for 10 percent of origination, 85 percent of being in charge, and 5 percent of collections. There can be arguments over these percentages that sometimes have to be decided by a managing partner or section leader. There is also some scamming if someone leaves in the middle of the year. Who gets his percentages?

A subgroup of the compensation committee ranks all 300+ partners in our firm. They have a huge spreadsheet with a line for each person. They are supposed to look at sustained performance over a period of time and whether the trajectory is up or not. This spreadsheet is broken down by the fourteen point scales.

There are fifteen people on the compensation committee, and they meet for three full days in February or March. They start at the top of the list and decide upon the number of points the person should have as well as his or her bonus. They have already been told by the executive committee how much is to be awarded for each point.

People at the bottom sometimes get screwed as we have run out of points. We will go back through the list to see if there are any aberrations. Twenty percent of attorneys appealed the decision last year. You generally go up or down only one tier a year. A tier is twenty points. If you are not doing well, they can ratchet you down or fire you.

Ten percent of the associates got bonuses last year. The local person or leader decides upon the amount. This amount can range from $2,500 to $10,000.

It takes seven to eight years to move from associate to partner. Some firms require that partners put capital into the firm. We require 25 percent of your salary to be put into a capital account, so an $800,000 partner must put $200,000 in. We work with a bank so that partners can borrow the money. We have a special arrangement that the firm pays the interest on these loans. However, when you leave the firm, the firm can take up to three years to repay you the amount in the capital account while you now have to pay interest on the loan. The chair sometimes forgives the interest if the person is taking a government job.

There are also automatic bonuses based upon billable hours. Associates are supposed to bill 1,950 hours a year, and partners are supposed to bill 1,850 hours. If you exceed your hours, you can get a bonus of $10,000 for associates or $25,000 for partners.

Doing pro bono work does not pay you a dime.

He refused the $10 payment for participation.

Lester is a compensation expert at one of the largest consulting firms in the United States. This is his story.

Partners have shares in the firm. Once you are appointed to being a partner, you automatically receive 120 shares (or points). There are six different levels of partners. The highest level is 420 shares. Within each of the six levels, the number of shares is identical, and each share is worth the same amount of money, so if a share is worth $100, the range of compensation is between $120,000 and $420,000. There is no other source of compensation for partners other than their shares. There are over 200 partners at our firm.

We distribute compensation depending upon profit at the end of the year. However, we distribute draws throughout the year depending upon projected profit. In theory, the projection could be wrong, and the partners would have to give money back. That has not occurred.

There is a partnership committee that determines if someone becomes a partner and whether or not they are promoted within the six levels. Another group determines how much each share is worth at the end of the year. Partners are supposed to progress through the different partnership levels. If they don't progress, they are released.

We have five different ranks for nonpartners ranging from principal to consultant. The base salary for these people is very much market driven. We compare our salaries to other firms. This is very important for recruiting and for keeping people. The salaries also differ a lot according to geography. For example, principals in New York in the energy business, the base salary will range from $100,000 to $150,000. It might only be $80,000 in Cleveland. At the lower level, a consultant will make $45,000 to $75,000 in New York, while the principal will make double that.

Therefore, the base salary is affected by rank, geography, and area of specialization.

Only people at the three highest levels are eligible for bonuses (except in the strategy group where everyone is eligible). Each person is ranked on a 1–4 scale, and a bonus is given to anyone with a 1, 2, or 3. Ninety-five percent of those eligible get some bonus with about one-third receiving a 1. The maximum bonus is 35 percent of the base salary. The percentage of bonus is also very much market driven.

We gather information about each person throughout the year, and then there is a very painful and difficult assessment done by various committees. These decisions are evaluated by other committees across and between departments. People then receive a single bonus check. The process is very time-consuming, but we strongly believe in fairness. It is left up to the supervisor on how to inform the person. Employees are supposed to be evaluated by their supervisor, but this can be very uneven.

The number of partners is limited. For most nonpartner ranks, it is not up and out. For some specialties, the employee must progress through the ranks or they are released. For other specialties, people can stay for many, many years. Again, this process is very much market driven.

Please send the $10 to a charity.

The narratives in this chapter reveal some commonalities among those who are attracted to jobs that pay commissions. People who prefer to make commissions tend to express a satisfaction with the sense of control that commission-based compensation provides. They often mention an affinity for having their pay reflect their work effort. Sales representatives tend to talk about the role of relationships in their work and compensation. One factor that pervades commission-based employment that is mentioned infrequently but is increasingly important as economic circumstances are currently quite tenuous is the issue of earnings in a down economy. The workforce on the cutting-edge of economic growth has a long way to fall when confronted with a brick wall.

NOTE

1. Continuing Medical Education training (CME) is required of all physicians.

Conclusions

"There is a whole culture to commission sales," as Lorenzo who worked on commission at a Circuit City in Michigan noted. That culture may be "cut-throat" or like a "shark tank." The culture in a commission system might also be described as a "team" where sales associates "work together." The commission structure, workforce dynamics, and management interact in a manner that people interpret and describe as the "culture" of the work environment. These factors reflect that culture and impact the efficacy of the commission system. The structure of the commission system, the culture of the organization, and the craft of management influence the success of the organization, or alternatively send it possibly into bankruptcy and liquidation.

Culture is not entirely independent from the structure of the commission system or the craft of management. The commission structure orients the competition and sets the boundaries of autonomy for the sales staff. The culture impacts whether that autonomy results in slack or increased productivity. And, management craft shades the culture, helps shape the perceptions, and along with the structure and culture determine job satisfaction. The employee perspective reveals that competence, trustworthiness, and goodwill when consistently and practically applied reinforce the commission structure in ways that enhance sustainability.

RANGE OF COMMISSIONS

There is also a range of commissions. Some jobs that appear almost identical have vastly different commission structures. For example, some clothing stores are structured around commissions, while others have no commission at all. Some stores make modifications to the structure from year to year, and others have made massive changes. For example, Circuit City went from a commission-based to an hourly-based structure before going out of business.

Different industries seem to have different commission structures. For example, most car salespeople receive a percentage (20 to 40 percent) of the profit made by the dealer. Those who sell clothing, jewelry, and cosmetics usually received a percentage of sales (1 to 10 percent). Realty companies representing house buyers and sellers usually split commissions equally (5 to 6 percent) with specific agents receiving a percentage (50 to 70 percent) of the commission from their companies. Commissions for the sales of appliances and electronic goods had greater complexity. The commission could vary by product and manufacturer and was often tied to a complex tier system. Similarly, salespeople in insurance would get a different percentage for different types of insurance, and this percentage could be quite different for renewals.

Some commission structures are affected by seniority and choice. For example, more senior real estate agents usually get a higher percentage of the commission (e.g., 60 percent instead of 50 percent) from the sale of a property. Seniority also seems to positively affect commission percentages for some insurance salespeople. There is also a trade-off that some realtors and hair stylists (see the companion volume, chapter 14) can voluntarily make. Sometimes one can "rent a desk" or "rent a booth" and keep a larger percentage of the commission.

KNOWLEDGE OF COMPENSATION STRUCTURE

It was somewhat surprising that almost half of those who earned commissions or bonuses reported they had little idea of how they were structured. Some complained about the complexity of the system, especially in the electronics industry. The fact that several respondents spontaneously said they did not care about the commission structure, ignored all "specials," and simply did what was best for the customer was another interesting and perhaps unexpected finding. On the flip side, several respondents kept all information on commissions in Excel spreadsheets. Others would check the details of every line on a commission statement. Understanding which workers are motivated by commissions and which are motivated by "a job well done" has tremendous benefit to managers.

THE DRAW SYSTEM

Most people on commission were not on straight commission. Some had a base salary, and others used some variant of the draw system. A draw gave a person a base salary if their commission was low in a given period. Sometimes the salesperson would have to pay back the draw or part of the draw in a subsequent pay period. It is somewhat fascinating that many of the people on straight commission looked down on people who received a draw or expressed disdain for the draw system. They would brag that they never needed to use the draw or implied that the person who relied up the draw did not have the guts to be a real salesperson. There was a considerable degree of competiveness expressed in the discussions of draws.

JOB SATISFACTION

The focus of this book is commissions and bonuses. However, the first question asked of the respondents was whether or not they liked their job and why. This question serves two purposes. First, the question is intended to put people at ease. Most people do not like to talk about their compensation. They are more willing to talk about their pay after they talk about what they do for work and what they think about it.

Second, what people think and how they feel about their work is fascinating. Asking about commissions and bonuses frames the discussion of what they think about their jobs. Similarly, respondents often talked about their compensation structure in terms of whether it led to a positive or negative work experience. Questions about whether they like their job, what they do at their job, and how they receive their compensation became integrated.

It was surprising that so many people actually like their jobs. Approximately 90 percent of respondents expressed satisfaction with their job.[1] Factors that affected this included:

- relating to people such as coworkers, managers, and customers;
- the pay;
- the compensation structure;
- the conditions of the work; and
- the nature of the work.

Respondents often pointed to people they related to as reasons for liking or disliking their jobs. This type of reason was the most common basis by which people evaluated their work. Below are selected quotes that highlight the sentiment of those who like their jobs because of the people or work environment:

- There were a lot of people to make friends with. [Logan at Dell]
- I love what I do. I get to see new people every day and I get to solve people's wants every day. It is great to see their eyes light up when I put a package together. [Daniel at Sound Advice/Tweeter]

- I love it. The dealership is like a family. We are all close. It is not competitive here. We are a team. It really is a family business. [Dorothy on selling Volvos]
- I love what I do. I interact with people on a daily basis. I help people. They get the cash they need in a bad economy. [Kal commenting on his commissions for buying jewelry]
- I love this job. I love Italy, and I get to go twice a year. [Larry, a travel consultant]
- I get to work with construction guys and play with big toys. It is a lot of fun. [Charles, who rents construction equipment]
- I like what I do. It is not boring. It is always a challenge. [Bernard, who processes contracts for Verizon]
- I like the job because it is not a 9 to 5 job. I have an interest in technology, and it is fun to be cutting-edge. It is a fascinating process dealing with the government. The days go quickly. [Edward, who sells communication equipment to the federal government]

Similarly, Brian became good friends with some of his customers while he sold jewelry. Patti liked meeting people selling cosmetics for Mary Kay. Robin enjoyed meeting people selling insurance. Tanisha liked selling clothes at Ann Taylor because it was low stress, and Janet liked being a financial advisor because it was fast paced. Some people simply like the work. Samuel, at Radio Shack, loves solving the problems that the "little old ladies" brought in. "It's fun," he said. Charles, who works for an executive search firm, loves the variety of work and that it is always interesting. Kent loves his work as a literary agent, in part, because he loves books. Richard loves doing loan processing because it is like solving puzzles.

Below are some quotes from people who disliked their jobs because of the people with whom they worked or the work environment.

- There was a lot of pressure to sell and be the first to greet the person entering the store. It was hard to be friends with your coworkers. [Betsy at Ralph Lauren]
- I did not like the work. The business was dishonest. There were also salespeople who would tell the customer that the service was free when it was not. A lot of salespeople were trying to get promoted into better positions and that depended upon their sales volume. [Nancy at Bell South]

Likewise, Gail hated her job selling tanning salon memberships because coworkers got in her way and tried to steal her commissions. Landon said you could not trust the other brokers at Merrill Lynch, and you could have no friends. Rachael was quitting her job managing a hedge fund because the bank was too disorganized and understaffed. Jonathan stopped selling Toyotas because he was a car nut and "no one cared about the cars"; and most of the telemarketers disliked their job. They did not like selling on the telephone and feared rejection.

The pay, compensation structure, and having variable income were also reasons the respondents noted when explaining why they did or did not like their jobs. The following are some selected quotes from those who liked their jobs for that reason:

- I can make as much money as I want if I work hard. [Martha, who sold real estate]
- I like selling cars. I like the challenge. I control my own income. [Hector on selling Hondas]
- The commission really helped. It created a sense of urgency. I felt I needed to take control of what was going on. [Max at a video store]
- I like the motivation of being the best employee I can be. I don't like to be lazy. Commissions are good for me. [Jack, who sold ice]
- I like what I do. I like my independence, and I control my own income. [Nolan on selling windows]
- I like working on commission because I basically write my own check. I get paid when I work hard. [Barry, regarding selling cruise packages]

Similarly, Roman loved selling phones for Verizon because there was the potential to make a lot of money. Megan liked selling advertising because she wrote her own paycheck, and Daniel liked doing event management for nonprofits because of the "thrill of the chase." Others liked being independent and feeling they had a lot of control over their own income. Many people on commission inferred that it was like they were self-employed and had tremendous control over their own schedules and earning potential.

There were several respondents who had a number of jobs over the years involving commissions and bonuses. They seemed to gravitate toward positions that gave them a certain type of adrenaline rush and sense of control. They thrived on the competition with others and within themselves. The sentiment may be best captured by the statement made by Billie at Nordstrom's when he responded that the "sky is my limit." Dorothy had a noncommission job at one point and said, "I like commission work. I worked for Best Buy for two months. After two months, I was number two in the country at selling warranties. It did not affect my paycheck. It drove me nuts."

Others did not care for work that had variable income. One salesperson working in a clothing store said she was happy for the hourly wage. However, her main job was studying for school, so she was not focused on the commission. A woman who sold bras to cancer victims said she did not have the proper aggression to be a salesperson, hated what she did, but needed the job. A respondent who used to work selling jewelry on commission was now very happy to do noncommission sales and now does not have the "urge to make quota." A person who used to work at Circuit City for commission became happy when they went to a straight hourly wage and believed his work improved as he now did other activities (stocking shelves and cleaning) to help the store in other ways.

SUMMARY

The commissions-based sales force is at the "cutting-edge" of economic growth. In other words, the motivation and ability of sales personnel to increase consumption can spur growth in a sector. This book is intended to analyze the experiences of those who receive commissions within and across various contexts to understand how sharp that edge may cut. Because incentive plans are crucial to attracting and retaining sales staff and have a major impact on the activities and behavior of salespeople, understanding how people relate to the commission structure is integral to calculating the appropriate investment in the sales force. The experiences of those who work for commissions teach us that commission structures interact with the dynamics of the workforce and the skill of management to elicit specific behaviors from sales staff. However, fostering competition or facilitating cooperation among sales staff is significantly more difficult to manage as this aspect seems to be more a function of how people come together within the policy structure of the company. Employers may use employee perspectives to gauge the work environment and determine how the structure of the commission system may yield the greatest gains in performance. Yet, the operation and administration of the commission system remains an artful aspect of management.

Another noteworthy contribution of this study has to do with what it reveals about the dilemmas of management. In the best-case scenario, skilled management and a well-designed commission structure cannot solve all the dilemmas of management simultaneously. For example, structuring the commission system to promote the broad company goal of increasing sales in the most profitable products may limit the extent to which commission may serve as an incentive. Alternatively, severing the cut of a sales force that grows out of proportion to company profits may change the dynamics of the workforce, possibly cutting out the highest-performing sales associates. In this case, the cutting-edge becomes so sharp that it cuts into company profits, often requiring severance of the sharp edge. The cutting-edge may be more dull, but the company is more likely to sustain growth. The true art of management is maximizing the big picture while still maintaining a work environment that allows for the retention of the highest-performing employees.

An obsession with sales to the exclusion of quality, customer service, and sustainability can have detrimental effects. An adequately structured commission system provides clear incentives without undermining trust. A well-designed incentive structure supported by management skilled in the craft of facilitating an organizational culture in which integrity is rewarded as much as sales numbers contribute to the sustainability of the organization. Sales for bonuses and commissions and consumption for its own sake is not only mindless. It is unsustainable.

NOTE

1. The National Opinion Research Center—General Social Survey found that in 2006, 55.9 percent of Americans were completely or very satisfied with their jobs and 29.9 percent were fairly satisfied.

References

Axelrod, Robert. 1984. *The Evolution of Cooperation*. New York: Basic Books.

Bowles, Samuel, and Herbert Gintis. 2004. "The Evolution of Strong Reciprocity: Cooperation in Heterogeneous Populations." *Theoretical Population Biology* 65(1):17–28.

Camerer, Colin F. 2003. *Behavioral Game Theory: Experiments in Strategic Interaction*. New York: Russell Sage Foundation.

Cook, Karen S., and Russell Hardin. 2001. "Norms of Cooperativeness and Networks of Trust." In Michael Hechter and Karl-Dieter Opp (eds.), *Social Norms*, 327–47. New York: Russell Sage Foundation.

Darlin, Damon. 2006. "The Last Stand of the 6-Percenters?" *New York Times* (September 3, 2006).

Dixit, Avinash, and Susan Skeath. 2004. *Games of Strategy*. New York: Norton.

Drolet, Aimee L., and Michael W. Morris. 2000. "Rapport in Conflict Resolution: Accounting for How Face-to-Face Contact Fosters Mutual Cooperation in Mixed-Motive Conflicts." *Journal of Experimental Social Psychology* 36:26–50.

Elton, Edwin J., Martin J. Gruber, Sanjiv Das, and Matthew Hlavka. 1993. "Efficiency with Costly Information: A Reinterpretation of Evidence from Managed Portfolios." *Review of Financial Studies* 6(1):1–22.

Fehr, Ernst, and Simon Gächter. 2000. "Fairness and Retaliation: The Economics of Reciprocity." *Journal of Economic Perspectives* 14(2):159–81.

Fleishman, Sandra. 2005. "Agents Aplenty: Career Jumpers Looking for Easy Commissions Make Low Percentage Play." *Washington Post*, December 18, 2005.

Fletcher, June, and Ruth Simon. 2006. "The New Word in Home Sales: 'Canceled.'" *Wall Street Journal* (November 3, 2006), W1.

Hill, Carolyn, and Laurence E. Lynn, Jr. 2008. *Public Management: A Three-Dimensional Approach*. Washington, DC: CQ Press.

Ho, Karen. 2009. *Liquidated: An Ethnography of Wall Street*. Durham, NC: Duke University Press.

Honey, M. 1987. "The Interview as Text: Hermeneutics Considered as a Model for Analyzing the Clinically Informed Research Interview." *Human Development* 30:69–82.

Kiewiet, D. Roderick, and Mathew D. McCubbins. 1991. *The Logic of Delegation: Congressional Parties and the Appropriations Process*. Chicago: University of Chicago Press.

Lewis, Michael. 1989. *Liar's Poker*. New York: W.W. Norton.

Loomis, Jack. 1959. "Communication, the Development of Trust, and Cooperative Behavior." *Human Relations* 12:305–15.

Miller, Gary, and Andrew B. Whitford. 2002. "Trust Incentives in Principal-Agent Negotiations." *Journal of Theoretical Politics* 14(2):231–67.

Seltzer, Richard. 2005. "Nonresponse in Telephone Surveys: The Reporting of Outcome Measures." American Statistical Association, *2005 ASA Proceedings*. A version of this article was given as a paper at the 2005 AAPOR conference.

Shea, Shawn. 1998. *Psychiatric Interviewing: The Art of Understanding*. New York: Saunders.

Valley, Kathleen L., Joseph Moag, and Max Bazerman. 1998. "A Matter of Trust: Effects of Communication on the Efficiency and Distribution of Outcomes." *Journal of Economic Behavior and Organizations* 34:211–38.

Zoltners, Andris A., Prabhakant Sinha, and Greggor A. Zoltners. 2001. *The Complete Guide to Accelerating Sales Force Performance*. New York: Amacom.

Index

About the Authors

Richard Seltzer is professor of political science at Howard University. His most recent books with The Rowman & Litttlefield Publishing Group are *Experiencing Racism: Exploring Discrimination through the Eyes of College Students* (with Nicole Johnson) and *Contemporary Controversies and the American Racial Divide* (with Robert Smith).

Holona LeAnne Ochs is assistant professor of political science at Lehigh University. She received her doctorate in political science from the University of Kansas, her master's degree in clinical marriage and family therapy, and bachelor's degree in psychology from Kansas State University. She was awarded the Howard Baumgartel Peace and Justice Award in 2007 and has published her research on social justice and governance in journals including *Justice Research and Policy Journal of Public Affairs Education, Policy Studies Journal, Social Science Quarterly*, and *American Politics Research.*

Breinigsville, PA USA
06 September 2010
244839BV00003B/9/P

9 780739 144398